OUTDOOR
SCHOOL

An imprint of Macmillan Publishing Group, LLC
120 Broadway, New York, NY 10271
OddDot.com

Library of Congress Control Number: 2020021773
ISBN 978-1-250-23084-3

OUTDOOR SCHOOL LOGO DESIGNER Tae Won Yu
COVER DESIGNER Tae Won Yu & Tim Hall
INTERIOR DESIGNER Tim Hall
EDITOR Nathalie Le Du
ILLUSTRATOR Aliki Karkoulia

Art from *Golden Guides: Birds* by James Gordon Irving. Art from *Golden Guides: Bird Life* and *Golden Guides: Poisonous Animals* by John D. Dawson. Art from *Golden Guides: Butterflies and Moths* by Andre Durenceau. Art from *Golden Guides: Sky Observers* by John Polgreen. Art from *Golden Guides: Trees* by Dorothea Barlowe. Golden Guides are published by Macmillan Publishing Group, LLC. Photos © Shutterstock

Our books may be purchased in bulk for promotional, educational, or business use. Please contact your local bookseller or the Macmillan Corporate and Premium Sales Department at (800) 221-7945 ext. 5442 or by email at MacmillanSpecialMarkets@macmillan.com.

Printed in China by 1010 Printing International Limited,
North Point, Hong Kong

First edition, 2021
1 3 5 7 9 10 8 6 4 2

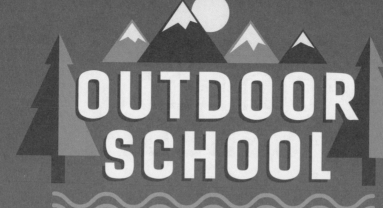

OUTDOOR SCHOOL

HIKING

AND

CAMPING

JENNIFER PHARR DAVIS
AND HALEY BLEVINS

ILLUSTRATED BY
ALIKI KARKOULIA

Odd Dot New York

OUTDOOR SCHOOL

OPEN YOUR DOOR.
STEP **OUTSIDE.**
YOU'VE JUST WALKED INTO
OUTDOOR SCHOOL.

Whether you're entering an urban wilderness or a remote forest, at Outdoor School we have only four guidelines.

→ **BE AN EXPLORER, A RESEARCHER, AND—MOST OF ALL—A LEADER.**

→ **TAKE CHANCES AND SOLVE PROBLEMS AFTER CONSIDERING ANY RISKS.**

→ **FORGE A RESPECTFUL RELATIONSHIP WITH NATURE AND YOURSELF.**

→ **BE FREE, BE WILD, AND BE BRAVE.**

We believe that people learn best through doing. So we not only give you information about the wild, but we also include three kinds of activities:

TRY IT → Read about the topic and experience it right away.

TRACK IT ↘ Observe and interact with the wildlife, and reflect on your experiences right in this book.

TAKE IT TO THE NEXT LEVEL ↗ Progress to advanced techniques and master a skill.

Completed any of these activities? Awesome! Check off your accomplishment and write in the date.

✓ **I DID IT!** DATE:

This book is the guide to the adventures you've been waiting for. We hope you'll do something outside your comfort zone—but we're not telling you to go out of your way to find danger. If something seems unsafe, don't do it.

And don't forget: This book is **YOURS**, so use it. Write in it, draw in it, make notes about your favorite waterfall hike in it, dry a flower in it, whatever! The purpose of Outdoor School is to help you learn about your world, help you learn about yourself, and—best of all—help you have an epic adventure.

So now that you have everything you need—keep going. Take another step. And another. And never stop.

Yours in adventure,

THE **OUTDOOR SCHOOL** TEAM

CONTENTS

🚶 PART II: HIKING 85

⛺ PART III: SET UP CAMP 191

✚ PART V: SURVIVAL   367

PART I

PLANNING
AND
PREPARATION

What would YOU do?

You are out on a day hike in the

heat of summer, and after two miles you stop for a snack and water break. You put your water bottle down for a second and whoops—it tumbles over, and all your water for the day spills out. Your plan was to hike five more miles on a trail that loops back to the parking lot. You packed a water filter, but you're not sure whether there are any water sources near the trail. After checking your map, you discover that there is a small stream, but it's three miles ahead. You could turn back to the parking lot now or hike ahead and maybe find water—it is summer, so that stream may have dried up. Perhaps you'll pass other hikers and can ask whether they have water to share. What would you do?

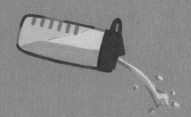

PLAN YOUR NEXT ADVENTURE

CHAPTER 1

Research

The best part of hiking is being outside and exploring, but researching can help you pick the coolest gear, pack the tastiest snacks, and plan the most scenic route.

To start, you need to decide where you want to hike. And choosing the right hike starts with resources such as a map, a guidebook, an internet search, or word of mouth.

MAP A map will show the length, route, and destination of a hike.

GUIDEBOOK A guidebook will give you a more detailed description of the route, information about the surrounding environment, and directions for making important turns.

INTERNET SEARCH Looking for a hike online can turn up a wide variety of options. You can narrow your search with keywords like "great views," "waterfalls," or "swimming hole." Check a few different sites to make sure the information is accurate and recent, or call the contact number if one is listed.

WORD OF MOUTH Talk with friends who like to hike and camp. They might tell you about a special rock formation just off the trail that's not on the map. Or they might tell you not to hike in a certain area when it's raining because of how muddy it can be. Making friends with hikers and campers is a great way to become a hiker and camper.

Now that you have your resources handy, here are some tips for picking the right trail:

→ When you are getting started, look for a trail that isn't too long or hard. You want to build your skills and your stamina before taking on the toughest trails.

→ Consider the best time of the day and the best time of the year to tackle your hike. You probably don't want to opt for that high elevation hike in the middle of a snowy winter nor do you want to hike on a desert trail in the heat of the day.

→ The average hiker hikes about 1.5–2 miles per hour (2.4–3.2 kilometers per hour). You may find that you like to hike as fast as possible or slowly saunter down the trail, but be conservative in the planning stages. Don't plan a ten-mile hike unless you want to be out in the wild for five to seven hours.

→ Don't just consider the distance; think about the terrain as well. A three-mile hike up a steep mountain will be far more difficult and take more time than a three-mile hike beside a river.

→ Think about what to expect in terms of the weather and animals you might encounter. If you don't like bugs, you are better off hiking in the winter. But if you don't like cold, then set out in the summer (and pack your bug spray).

→ Remember that the weather at high elevations can be drastically different and there may be lingering snow and ice or a winter storm at any time of year.

→ Research the organization or land management group that is in charge of the trail. Is the hike in a local park or on a county greenway? Does it go through a national forest or a state park? Locate a phone number or website for the organization that manages the trail and make a call to check for potential closures, restrictions, or necessary permits.

CLOSURES AND PERMITS

Some hiking trails require a special permit, and trails might be closed for repairs or because of bad weather. It is disappointing to spend time and energy preparing for a hike only to see a big CLOSED sign when you get there. Call or visit the website for the authority in charge of the trail to check for recent updates and information on permit requirements.

TRY IT → Find Your Pace

STEP 1 Find a place where you can walk for thirty minutes. It could be around your neighborhood, on a school track, or on a trail or greenway.

MILES	TIME
1.2 miles	30 min.
2.4 miles	60 min.

STEP 2 If you need a friend or parent to come with you, find a walking buddy as well.

STEP 3 When you are ready to start, set your timer and distance tracker to zero.

STEP 4 Walk for 30 minutes at a normal pace.

STEP 5 At the end of thirty minutes, check your distance and multiply it by two. The resulting number tells you how many miles you might walk in an hour.* Once you know the average miles per hour you can hike, it will be easier to plan how much time you might need on a trail.

* If you tracked your distance on a track, sidewalk, or paved surface, you can expect your miles per hour to go down by a half mile or more once you hit the trail. The uneven terrain will slow you down a bit, and there will be more cool things to look at, like plants, views, and wildlife.

I DID IT! DATE:

The Good-to-Go Checklist

➤ A map or guidebook, internet access, and a friend or two.

Here's a checklist to make sure you are good to go. Use it for your next hike and return to it as a template for future adventures.

☐ Look at your map or guidebook and pick a trail that you want to explore.

☐ Write the name of the park, forest, or nature preserve where the hike is located. (Look closely: Sometimes trails cross over several different properties or land management regions.)

☐ Circle the features you think you will see on your hike:

STREAM   **LAKE**   **WATERFALL**   **BEACH**   **MOUNTAIN**

☐ Given the features chosen above, what gear will you need?

☐ Write the hike distance. How many miles/kilometers is it?

☐ Divide the hike distance (in miles/kilometers) by your personal pace or 1.5 (2.4 for km). The result is a good estimate of how many hours to plan for the hike.

☐ Ask your friends if they have ever been on the trail that you are planning to hike. What was it like for them? What can you learn from their experiences that might make your hike better?

I DID IT! DATE:

Research an Overnight Backpacking Trip

Once you become comfortable planning day hikes, you can
start prepping for overnight backpacking trips. Here are a
few things to consider when creating a plan, or itinerary, for a
multiday trip:

- Overnight packs are heavier than day packs and will
  cause you to hike more slowly.

- Make sure you plan to stop for the night in an area that
  allows camping and, if necessary, that you have the
  proper permit for the campsite.

- Are you cooking? If so, you probably want to camp near a
  water source.

I DID IT! DATE:

LEAVE AN ITINERARY

Before you head out on any trail, always leave your
itinerary with someone. Even if you don't know exactly
which route you will hike, leave the name of the trailhead
and how long you will be gone. That way if you run
into trouble and don't return when you are
expected, someone will know where to look
for you. This could be even more important if
you encounter treacherous weather.

CHAPTER 2

Packing

Once you decide on the route, you will have a better idea of what to pack. For example, if you are hiking an exposed trail (a path located away from the protection of trees and natural shade or barriers) and you are headed out in the heat of the summer, then you can pack a small umbrella to provide shade. (You can also start early in the morning or later in the day to avoid the highest temperatures.)

The conditions you need to prepare for and the items you need to carry will vary greatly based on the time of year, difficulty of the trail, and weather forecast.

Start with these questions to get a better idea of what to pack and what to expect on the trail:

1. WHAT HAS THE WEATHER BEEN DOING?

Several prior days of rain or freezing temps can affect the trail even if you have a warm, sunny day to hike. You might need to prepare for mud, snow, ice, fallen trees, or flooding before you leave home. If it has been hot and dry, you'll need to prepare for scarce or poor-quality water sources.

2. WHAT IS THE WEATHER FORECAST?

Prepare for the anticipated weather. The proper rain gear and warm layers can turn a rainy or cold hike into a comfortable adventure, as opposed to a hypothermic slog.

3. WHAT ARE THE LOWEST AND HIGHEST TEMPERATURES YOU CAN EXPECT?

It is not uncommon for weather to change quickly, and sometimes it can feel like you have experienced four seasons on one hike. Bring lightweight clothing layers that you can quickly adjust to help stay comfortable.

4. IS IT BUG SEASON?

It doesn't matter how beautiful the view; if your head is surrounded by buzzing, biting insects, then it's hard to enjoy. Consider packing long sleeves and bug spray or a bug net to go over your head if you expect insects.

5. WHAT ANIMALS ARE OUT THERE?

Animals can often influence what you take as well as when and where you hike. If you are hiking in Yellowstone National Park, add bear spray to your pack. However, if you are in New England and hoping to spot a moose from the trail, plan a hike for earlier or later in the day when moose tend to be more active.

6. WHAT WILL THE TERRAIN BE LIKE?

If you are planning to hike a trail that is steep and rocky, add hiking poles and gaiters to your packing list. (Don't confuse gaiters with gators. You shouldn't hike with a large reptile in rocky terrain! Instead, look for ankle sleeves that cover the top of your shoe, sock, and calf. These gaiters can help keep pebbles and debris out of your shoes and keep you more comfortable.)

7. WHAT IS THE ELEVATION?

The higher you climb, the more likely you are to encounter severe temperatures and exposed terrain. Add extra clothes and sunscreen for high-elevation hikes. You also need to be prepared for snow and ice any time of the year in high mountains.

8. ARE THERE ANY RESUPPLY POINTS?

Some trails pass visitor centers, stores, and other places where you can refill your water or buy a snack. These resupply points are more important on backpacking trips than day hikes. But don't underestimate the value of planning an ice cream break as part of a long outing!

TRY IT →

Pack Your Perfect Pack

WHAT YOU'LL NEED

➢ A day pack and some hiking essentials

STEP 1 Rummage through your house to find these basic essentials that you will need on every hike:

COMFORTABLE SHOES AND HIKING SOCKS

QUICK-DRYING ATHLETIC CLOTHING

A BACKPACK TO CARRY EVERYTHING LISTED BELOW

SNACKS

MAP

PLENTY OF WATER

COMPASS

LIGHT RAIN PROTECTION SUCH AS A JACKET OR PONCHO

AN EXTRA LAYER OF CLOTHING FOR ADDED WARMTH

FIRST AID KIT

STEP 2 Once you collect all your necessary gear, put everything on or place it inside your pack. Make sure your water, snacks, map, and compass are in an accessible place in your pack (not at the bottom) or in your pockets so that you don't have to spend time digging for them.

STEP 3 Put on the pack and walk around outside. Is your pack comfortable? Does it feel heavy? Can you make any adjustments to make it fit better?

I DID IT! DATE:

TRACK IT ↘ Pick and Pack the Extras

You have collected all the items that you need to take on a hike. Now write down what else you want to bring. Perhaps this book, a wildflower identification book, a phone, or a watercolor set?

1.

2.

3.

4.

5.

You may want to bring a cooler full of snacks and five of your favorite books. But remember, you have to carry everything that you bring with you. Look back over your packing list. Is there anything you can cross out?

➢ When you go camping and backpacking you will also have to spend more time planning your gear list. What are some pieces of additional gear that you would need to bring on an overnight trip?

I DID IT! DATE:

CHAPTER 3

Training for the Trail

You've collected your maps and researched the trail you want to hike, you've made an itinerary for the trip and packed up all your gear, but are *you* ready? Like, physically able to do this particular hike?

You don't have to be in great shape to go for a hike. That's one of the best parts of the trail—you can go as slow or as fast as you want. There is not a right or wrong pace. But, the hikers who get in shape before they hit the trail typically enjoy it more and have the option of going farther. There is a big difference between feeling good while climbing a big hill or needing to stop every few steps to catch your breath.

If you need or want to get in better shape for the trail, use these hiking-specific fitness suggestions to increase your strength and endurance.

Go for a Walk.... Now

Walk your neighborhood to establish a fitness and mileage base. If your parents, friends, or neighbors like to go for walks, then ask if you can join them. Do you have a dog? Is your mom always asking you to take it for walks? Well, this is your opportunity to get in shape and earn some brownie points. Or better yet—start a pet walking service to get in shape and make some money, too.

Get Your Heart Pumping

Walking around your neighborhood usually isn't as difficult as hiking on a trail with roots and rocks, climbs and descents, so you also want to include some activity that gets your heart rate up more than just walking. Simply play sports, go for a run, ride a bike, jump rope, or break up your homework with some jumping jacks.

BURPEE If you want a challenge, see how many burpees you can do. No, that is not burping at the dinner table. A burpee starts with a push-up, then you hop your feet up to your fingers and jump as high as you can into the sky. It sounds simple enough, but a couple of these can wear you out. Hold a burpee competition with a sibling or parent to push yourself—and them!

Increase Strength

Increasing strength is a great thing to do for your hiking adventures. Yes, hiking takes lots of endurance built on aerobic exercise, like swimming, running, and biking. But hiking up mountains and carrying a pack also require strong muscles! The good news is that you don't need a weight room or fitness coach to build muscle. Since hiking focuses on lower body strength, do squats, lunges, and wall sits to help increase your stamina for the trail.

SQUAT Start with your feet spread a little wider than your shoulders and slowly lower your bottom toward the ground as if you were sitting in an imaginary chair. Once you get the feel for this motion, do three sets of ten.

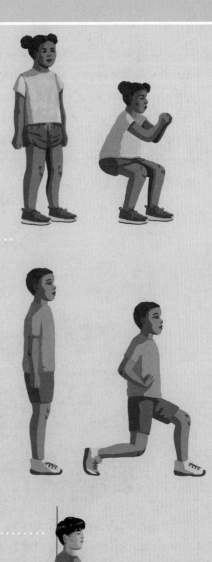

LUNGE Start standing. Take a big step with your left leg and drop your right knee toward the ground. Hold this position with your right knee a few inches above the ground for a few seconds, and then use your left leg to push off and bring your left and right feet back together again. Now put your right foot out and repeat. Can you do fifteen on each leg?

WALL SIT Pretend you are sitting in a chair, but place your back against a supporting wall or tree. Within a minute or two, your leg muscles will start to ache and maybe even shake!

Improve Balance and Flexibility

Crossing a creek on a fallen log with a pack on your back is akin to a gymnast walking across a balance beam.

And while you don't need Olympic-quality balance to hike, it helps to practice your balance before you hit the trail. The next time you are with a friend, make it a game to see who can balance on one foot the longest.

Increasing your flexibility is also a key component of becoming a hiker or backpacker. Flexibility can help you when you are scrambling up boulders or ducking under trees. Plus, working on your range of motion is one of the best ways to protect yourself from injuries when you fall or take missteps on the trail. The more comfortably your body can twist and turn, the less likely it is to get hurt. Learning yoga and incorporating a few positions into your daily routine is a great way to become more flexible and practice deep breathing before hitting the trail.

Here are two poses to get you started:

WARRIOR II This pose can help add flexibility to your core and strengthen your leg muscles. Start in a wide stance with both legs extended out to the side in a wide upside down V position. Now keep your left foot straight and turn your right foot out ninety degrees so the toes point perpendicular to the left foot. Turn to look over your right foot, take a deep breath, bend your knees slightly, and lift your arms up into a T position so they are outstretched straight from your body. Take another deep breath and shift your weight toward the front foot. Hold this position for several deep breaths and then repeat on the opposite side with your left foot turned out.

DOWNWARD-FACING DOG This is a great pose for stretching out tired hiking legs and keeping your glutes and hamstrings (aka your butt and thighs) loose and limber on the trail. You can enter this pose by reaching down and touching your toes. Now walk your hands in front of you until your body is in the shape of an upside-down V. Take several deep breaths and hold the pose as long as it is comfortable.

This ten-minute routine will help get you in better shape for the trail. You can do it indoors or outdoors (but it's better outdoors).

> **WHAT YOU'LL NEED**
>
> ➤ Your body, a jump rope, a clock or stopwatch, and comfortable workout clothes.

STEP 1 Look at the clock or start your stopwatch. Jump rope at a comfortable pace, about 50 percent of full effort for two minutes. At 50 percent effort you should still be able to sing out loud without much trouble—even if it's not pretty.

STEP 2 Lunge for two minutes. Instead of seeing how many you can do, focus on your form.

STEP 3 Plank for one minute. Put your hands on the ground and straighten the rest of your body on your toes, as if you are starting a push-up. When holding this position starts to get tough, focus on taking long, deep breaths.

STEP 4 Jump rope for two minutes and go a little faster than the first round, about 75 percent of full effort. At 75 percent effort it is difficult to sing out loud or hold a conversation, but you should be able to easily answer simple questions such as "What type of ice cream do you want to eat after this workout?"

STEP 5 Squat for two minutes. This is another exercise where you don't need to rush through it or see how many you can do; just make slow, steady movements and hold each squat for a few seconds before standing back up.

STEP 6 One minute left! Go all out and see how many times you can jump rope in the final sixty seconds. Give 100 percent, full effort for this last push. Full effort means there's no time to sing or think about ice cream. Just go as hard as you can!

GREAT JOB!

STEP 7 Great job! Take a deep breath and drink some water.

I DID IT! DATE:

TRACK IT ↘

Watch Your Progress

Practice your new fitness routine a few times each week, and track your fitness to show how your strength and endurance improve over time. Write down the best results from your exercise routine over the next three weeks.

1. How many times can you jump rope in a minute?

2. How long can you hold a wall sit?

3. How long can you hold a plank position?

4. How long can you balance on your right foot?

5. How long can you balance on your left foot?

WEEK 2

1. How many times can you jump rope in a minute?

2. How long can you hold a wall sit?

3. How long can you hold a plank position?

4. How long can you balance on your right foot?

5. How long can you balance on your left foot?

WEEK 3

1. How many times can you jump rope in a minute?

2. How long can you hold a wall sit?

3. How long can you hold a plank position?

4. How long can you balance on your right foot?

5. How long can you balance on your left foot?

I DID IT! DATE:

Race Into Shape

Hiking is great training for any physical activities such as sports, biking, or running. Consider signing up for a 5K or 10K race in your town. Hiking will help you get in shape for the race, and the race will help you get in shape for hiking.

I DID IT! DATE:

EASY NO-BAKE ENERGY BALLS

Here's a snack that is fun to make, packed with energy, and easy to take with you on the trail.

INGREDIENTS

2 cups instant oatmeal
½ cup honey
½ cup peanut butter (or other seed or nut butter)
1 ½ cups trail mix (use your favorite or make your own; see how on page 73)
a pinch of salt

DIRECTIONS

1. In a big bowl, stir all the ingredients together.
2. Place the bowl in the refrigerator for thirty minutes.
3. Remove the bowl from the fridge, and roll the mixture into balls about the size of golf balls.
4. Store your energy balls in the fridge or freezer until your next hike.

I DID IT! DATE:

SECTION 2

PACK
YOUR
GEAR

CHAPTER 4

The Big Three: Backpack, Sleeping Bag, Shelter

When backpackers talk about gear, they often refer to the Big Three—the three biggest and most important pieces of gear that you need on a backpacking trip:

1. BACKPACK

2. SLEEPING BAG

3. SHELTER

Backpack

Climbing a mountain, or even walking a few miles, would be difficult without a backpack. How would you carry your snacks, water, and extra clothes, and all your other gear? The size of your backpack will be determined by the length of your trip and what items you need to bring. If you are headed out for the day, you can bring a backpack that is only filled with the gear or items needed for that day, aka a day pack. If you are hiking for several days, or even weeks or months, you will want a larger backpack.

Your backpack capacity is measured in liters (rather than inches or centimeters). Liters measure how much space is inside of your pack, also known as the volume. You want to be able to fit all the essentials and not much more. (But just because you have extra space or volume in your pack, it doesn't mean you need to fill it. Remember, you have to carry everything you pack!)

There are two main types of backpacks, internal frame and external frame. The main difference between the two packs is that the metal support system that helps distribute the weight of your gear to your hips and shoulders is visible on an external frame model and it is located inside the pack fabric in an internal frame backpack.

EXTERNAL FRAME **INTERNAL FRAME**

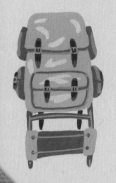

Internal frames are currently the most popular. A third option is a frameless pack. People who carry very little and try to hike fast often use this type.

Everyone is different, so try out different backpacks until you find the one that best fits you. Your torso length will determine what size you get—not how tall you are. The hip belt should sit on your hips so most of the weight rests there instead of on your shoulders. You don't want a backpack that is too heavy because you have to carry that weight! You also don't want a backpack that is so light that it doesn't have the proper structure or support system built-in to help you carry your load. Whenever you are trying on packs, load them up, adjust the straps to fit your body, and walk around! Most backpacks feel good when they are empty. But that can all change once they are stuffed to the gills.

Customize Your Backpack

There are plenty of ways you can make your pack more functional for your needs. Hikers take off extra cords, loops, etc., that they are not using. After all, that is just unnecessary extra weight. Add additional pockets to hold things that you use throughout the day like snacks, maps, phone, camera, and lip balm. So if a backpack doesn't come with hip-belt pockets (or maybe pockets that aren't very big), sew them on. Pockets can also be added to the shoulder straps—great for glasses or a phone. In addition to pockets, bungee cords and loops can be added for a variety of reasons. Some people hang water bottles off loops on their shoulder straps so they are easily accessible. It's also a visual reminder to drink frequently! And if you are carrying an umbrella and trekking poles, adding an attachment to hold the umbrella will allow you to still hike with your trekking poles.

TRY IT → Backpack Sizing

WHAT YOU'LL NEED

➢ A flexible tape measure, a partner, and a pencil or pen.

STEP 1 Tilt your head forward and find the largest bump at the base of your neck, between your shoulders. This is your C7 vertebra.

C7 VERTEBRA

STEP 2 Put your thumbs on your hips. Keep your thumbs on your hips and rotate your hands so your fingers make a straight line across your back. The spot where your fingers meet on your back is the bottom of your torso length.

STEP 3 Stand up straight and have your partner measure from the bony prominence at the top of your neck to the spot on your back that is even with your hip bones.

STEP 4 Record your torso length:

I DID IT! DATE:

Different backpack brands have different sizes based on torso length, but now you know what you are looking for. Also, if you go into an outdoor store, you can have an expert measure your torso length and see if you got the same number.

Sleeping Bag

Have you ever been on a camping trip and spent the night shivering instead of sleeping? The proper sleeping bag can help solve that problem. Sleeping bags are rated by degrees. The rating of the bag tells you the lowest temperature in which the bag will keep an average sleeper warm. You should choose a bag with a rating that is lower than the temperatures you expect to face. And if you get cold easily, keep that in mind! The sleeping bag you choose will have a lot to do with where you are hiking. If you are in a warm climate, you can take a higher degree bag. If you are visiting a cold climate, put a sleeping bag liner inside your bag to add extra warmth. It also helps keep your bag clean! And if you get too toasty, you can sleep on top of your bag and use the liner like a sheet.

Sleeping Pads

Pack a sleeping pad to provide a thin layer of warmth and insulation—and so you aren't sleeping directly on the ground. A sleeping pad is usually a foam pad or an air mattress that is often called a "blow-up" pad by hikers because you blow it up with your mouth and lungs before you sleep on it at night. The foam pads are more durable and can be kept on the outside of a pack to be used as a quick seat cushion during a snack break, but the air mattress has the ability to provide more loft and comfort.

The two most common types of sleeping bags are down and synthetic. Hikers often think of the warmth-to-weight ratio when buying a sleeping bag. No one likes a long, cold, miserable night. But you also have to carry every single item you put in your pack. So as cozy as a big, fluffy sleeping bag sounds, choose wisely.

DOWN VS. SYNTHETIC SLEEPING BAGS

	DOWN	SYNTHETIC	WINNER
Weight	Lighter	Heavier	**Down**
Compression (ability to crush into your pack)	Compressible	Not as compressible as down	**Down**
Potential allergen	Feathers make some people sneeze	Nonallergenic	**Synthetic**
Durability	Lasts a long time if you take really good care of it	Lasts a long time	**Synthetic**
Works when wet	Nope	Yep	**Synthetic**
Cost	Expensive	Affordable	**Synthetic**

Shelter: Tents, Tarps, Hammocks

Have you ever built a fort and slept in your backyard? Was it warm? Drafty? Did you get swarmed by insects? Were you comfortable? These are all things to think about when you are choosing a shelter.

If you want to be fully enclosed without any risk of insects or animals checking in on you in the middle of the night, then choose a tent. It usually comes with a rain fly—an outer tarp you put over the tent to be protected from rain. But if you choose to sleep with the rain fly off, you can stargaze while still being protected from those pesky mosquitoes!

A freestanding tent uses poles and can stand on its own. If you don't like where you pitched it—and you haven't staked it in yet—you can just pick it up and move it. (Imagine being able to move your house!) Tents tend to keep in the most heat. The downside is that you can wake up some mornings with condensation inside the tent.

Scoring the Perfect Tent

You want a shelter that is breathable and allows good air circulation. If sleeping under an open tarp is not your cup of tea, a good option for breathability and airflow is a double-wall tent with the rain fly off.

DOUBLE-WALL TENTS ▸ Double-wall tents have an inner structure typically made of lightweight silnylon and bug netting that can keep you zipped up from the outside world, but you have to add the rain fly or outer wall to make the shelter waterproof. Double-wall shelters are heavier than single-wall models and, like single wall tents, can be either freestanding or nonfreestanding, but with the rain fly on, they are sturdier in high winds and severe storms.

SINGLE-WALL TENTS ▸ Single-wall tents come in freestanding or nonfreestanding models. Single-wall models, with mesh windows and vents sewn into one layer of fabric, tend to be the lighter option, but they also tend to have less air circulation—and thus more condensation—than a double-wall tent.

FREESTANDING TENTS ▸ Freestanding tents do not need to be staked down to keep their structure, so once you set it up in one location, you can literally pick up the shelter and move it to a campsite ten feet away to catch a better sunset . . . or to get farther away from the guy camped nearby who just confessed to snoring like a chainsaw.

Regardless of which type of tent you have, the principles of setting up your outdoor home remain the same. And, if on the first try—or the second try, or the tenth try—the tent seems crooked and insecure, don't be discouraged. The real key to setting up a tent like a pro is to practice!

A tarp is lighter than most tents and is usually set up using hiking poles, lightweight rope called guylines, and tent stakes that you push into the ground to secure the tarp. Sometimes tarps are floorless, but there are now many options with bug netting, so your tarp can also be fully enclosed. If your tarp is open, be prepared for mosquito season! It also might feel drafty on cold nights. But you can set up a tarp in the rain without getting everything completely wet! Another advantage is how easy it is to throw up in the middle of the day if there's a sudden rainstorm or you need shade to escape the midday heat.

Have you ever relaxed in a hammock in the summer breeze? Maybe you even fell asleep? With a hammock, you don't have to worry about finding level ground or having rocks, sticks, or roots poking through the bottom of your tent. But you do need trees! If you are hiking in an area with plenty of trees, a hammock is a lightweight option for you. But if you're hiking in the desert, or above tree line—which means that you are at high altitude where few (if any) trees grow—you could put yourself in a tough situation!

Know the terrain before you set off. If you decide to hammock camp, you will also need to bring a tarp to provide protection in a rain or snowstorm.

Customize Your Shelter

You can save a lot of money by making your own gear. Instead of buying the groundsheet that goes with your tent, make your own out of Tyvek. Tyvek is a lot cheaper than the actual tent footprint and you can cut it to the size that best fits your tent or tarp. It's also great to put under your sleeping bag and pad if you are cowboy camping, that is, without a tent or tarp. And it's not just the groundsheet...You can modify your tent, too! Is water pooling in your entrance when it rains? Add a bungee cord that pulls your rain fly taut. Do you like using a tarp, but don't like getting bit by mosquitoes? Sew a bug net onto your tarp!

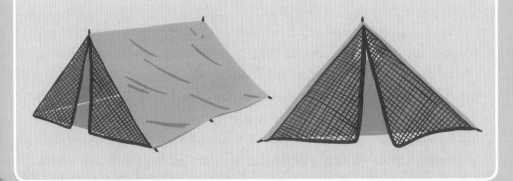

The Big Three Questionnaire

Use the questionnaire below to choose the best Big Three for your favorite hike or use it as a checklist for your next adventure.

Where will you be hiking?

What distance will you cover?

For how many days and nights will you be hiking?

What type of terrain will you experience? Will it be rocky, wet, or forested?

What are the likely temperatures?

What is the likely weather?

How much weight do you want to carry?

How much money do you want to spend on gear?

I DID IT! DATE:

CHAPTER 5

Clothing

One of the toughest things to predict in the wilderness is the weather. You might have an idea of what to expect. Or you might think you have an idea. You looked at the forecast and picked a day that was supposed to be dry, and halfway up the mountain, it starts to rain. Hey, even the weatherman gets it wrong sometimes! And sometimes the weather turns out to be just what you thought. The forecast said it would be cold. And it did feel cold...for the first twenty minutes. But then you started to put in some real effort as you gained elevation, and now you're drenched in sweat and stuck wearing a heavy sweater.

Boots on the Ground

In recent years, lightweight hiking shoes and trail sneakers have booted the traditional heavy, high-cut hiking boots out as the most popular trail shoes. *But* boots are still a great choice for hikers wanting more ankle support and extra protection from rocks or snow. If you decide to go with boots, spend plenty of time wearing them around the house and neighborhood to "break them in," a process that makes them more flexible and fitted to your foot, before you wear them on the trail.

BASE LAYER

MIDLAYER

OUTER LAYER

So just how do you pack for a hiking or backpacking trip in a range of conditions? The answer is layers.

When you are hiking in spring, summer, and fall, you can usually bring three layers for your upper body:

In the winter, you may need to add more for warmth.

Your base layer is very important because it is directly against your skin. It will play a large role in regulating your body temperature. Your base layer can be a short-sleeve shirt or a light long-sleeve shirt. Choose something that wicks sweat away from your body and dries quickly. There are synthetic and wool options for your base layer. Synthetic layers dry fast and are great at wicking sweat. But if you are going to be in the backcountry for multiple days, wool is better. Wool doesn't wick as well or dry as fast as synthetic materials, but it is antimicrobial, which keeps it from smelling as bad. It will also keep you warm even when it is wet.

TRY IT → Make Your Own Rain Poncho

Rain gear can be expensive, and after a while it loses its waterproofing. But garbage bags are cheap, so if your poncho rips, you can just make another one!

> **WHAT YOU'LL NEED**
> ➤ A garbage bag (a thick one is best), scissors, and possibly duct tape.

STEP 1 Cut a hole for your head in the center of the bag's bottom seam. Start small—you can always make the hole bigger.

STEP 2 Put the bag over your head to check the size of the hole. You should be able to get your head through without a problem, but it shouldn't be too big or water will get in. If you need to make it a bit smaller, you can close up the collar with a little duct tape, which will also increase the durability of your poncho.

STEP 3 Take the bag off and make two armholes, one on each side.

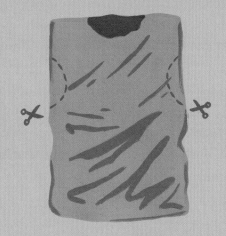

STEP 4 Put the poncho back on and make sure the armholes are the right size and in the correct location. Adjust as needed.

If you like your rain poncho, you can even try making a garbage bag rain skirt with a drawstring cinch waist to go with it!

I DID IT! DATE:

Cotton's Great. Unless You're Cold and Wet!

Have you heard the expression "cotton kills"? We usually sweat when we hike, and cotton absorbs that moisture and stays wet. If you sweat or get caught in the rain, the cotton will stick to your skin and pull the heat from your body. Once you start losing body heat, you risk hypothermia—your body temperature becomes too low for your organs to work properly.

The layer that goes on top of your base is called a midlayer. A midlayer is usually a type of fleece or midweight synthetic or wool top. This layer is often used when you start out on a chilly morning, stop for a break, or if you reach an elevation or spot where the wind picks up and you cool down. The great thing about layers is  you can take them off and put them back on all day. Paying attention to your body temperature and taking time to adjust as needed will pay off in the long run. If you use your layers appropriately, your hike will feel the most comfortable.

Your outer layer can be a variety of things, depending on where you are hiking and what the weather is like. Some people like to use a "puffy," or a jacket that is lightweight and warm. These jackets can be synthetic or made of down and are usually somewhat puffy (thus the name) and compressible. Others will use a rain jacket as an outer layer, especially in cold and wet conditions. A rain jacket can pull double duty as it will hold in body heat and keep you dry—and it also blocks the wind.

If it's summer, you might want to hike in shorts. But bring a pair of lightweight wind pants or rain pants as a second warming layer, if you expect high winds or rain. If the temperature is cold or it is wet, you should layer your legs like you do for your upper body. There are lightweight and midweight synthetic and wool bottoms. They can be worn over or under shorts if needed. If you are using rain pants, look for lightweight, breathable options.

Layers of Accessories

Layering doesn't just apply to your clothing. You can also add warmth by packing or putting on a few extra accessories. Here are a few to consider:

BASEBALL CAP OR SUN HAT FOR SHADE

BEANIE OR WARM WINTER CAP

BALACLAVA MASK

(This is fun to say and warm to wear. It's a sleeve for your neck and head with a cutout for your face.)

BANDANNA OR TUBULAR BANDANNA SUCH AS A BUFF

MITTENS OR GLOVES

COMPRESSION SLEEVES FOR ARMS AND LEGS

(Find this performance wear at cycling or running shops.)

GAITERS

TRY IT → Layer Up Like an Onion

Thin layers give you more options than heavy sweaters or bulky jackets.

STEP 1 Look in your closet and see what types of lightweight layers you already have.

STEP 2 See how many you can put on at one time. Try to get four or five different layers if you can! (For example, start with a tank top or T-shirt, then add a long-sleeve shirt, lightweight fleece, and a windbreaker or rain jacket.)

STEP 3 Go for a walk (a hike in the woods or a walk around your neighborhood).

STEP 4 Adjust your layers by taking them off or putting them back on so that you are perfectly comfortable the entire hike. Make it your goal to avoid sweating and shivering.

After a few walks, you will get a better idea of what combinations work best in different temperatures.

 **I DID IT!** DATE:

TRACK IT ↘ The Perfect Outfit

Found the perfect outfit for sun, snow, and everything in between? Write the details on the next page so you know the right combo for your next climb.

WALK 1   DATE: TIME:

WEATHER:

LAYERS:

NOTES:

WALK 2   DATE: TIME:

WEATHER:

LAYERS:

NOTES:

WALK 3   DATE: TIME:

WEATHER:

LAYERS:

NOTES:

I DID IT!   DATE:

45

CHAPTER 6

Camp Stove

Think about how great it is to come in after a chilly day outside and sip hot chocolate. Thanks to camp stoves, you can enjoy that same luxury even when you are backpacking! If you have ever camped in a drive-in campground or been to an outdoor barbecue, you are probably imagining large stoves that would be a lot of work to haul up a mountain. But backpacking stoves are quite light and fit easily inside your pack.

CANISTER STOVES The most common type of stove for backpacking is a canister stove. Canister stoves are lightweight and easy to use and bring water to a boil pretty fast. You also don't have to worry about spilling fuel because the fuel canister screws right into the stove. Most people consider this compact, easy-to-use stove a great option, but it can be difficult to find fuel if you are in a small town without an outdoor store.

LIQUID-FUEL STOVES A liquid-fuel stove is a good option if you will be in extreme cold because the heat provided by the liquid gas is extremely hot and can cook food faster than other types of stoves can.

These stoves use white gas—also known as camp fuel or naphtha—and work well if you need to melt snow for drinking or do a large amount of cooking. They are heavier and bulkier than canister stoves, but they have wider bases of support so they do not tip over easily, and the fuel is cheaper. These stoves are often more difficult to use than canister stoves, they can be more dangerous, and they also require more maintenance.

ALCOHOL STOVES Alcohol stoves are very inexpensive and incredibly light, plus fuel is easy to find. But they cook food slowly and don't work as well in windy or cold conditions. You have to be very careful when using an alcohol stove because even a small amount of spilled fuel can start a fire. They should not be used or operated by a novice hiker or anyone camping in dry and windy conditions or areas prone to wildfires.

ESBIT STOVES An Esbit stove uses fuel tabs instead of a liquid fuel, so you don't have to worry about a fuel spill!

These stoves are compact, but it will take a while to make your meal. Sometimes the fuel tabs have an odor and they can leave a sticky residue on your pot.

WOOD STOVES You have probably been around a campfire at some point. A wood stove is a more traditional stove option and kind of like having a mini campfire!

With a wood stove, you don't need to carry fuel because you use twigs and leaves. But just like a campfire, this cooking option will take more time and effort than the others. It could be tough to find dry wood after a long day of rain. Sometimes campfires and wood stoves are banned to prevent wildfires, and many campsites don't allow campfires at high elevation because of high winds and a lack of firewood, so research your park's rules.

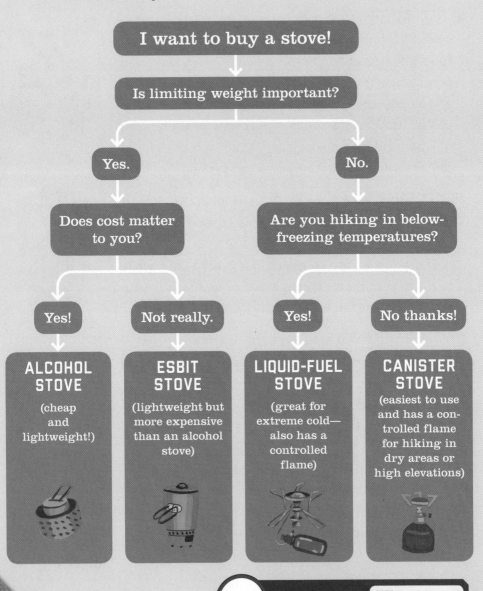

TRY IT →

Choose the Perfect Stove for You

Before you buy a stove, ask these questions to determine which is best for you.

I want to buy a stove!

Is limiting weight important?

Yes.

No.

Does cost matter to you?

Are you hiking in below-freezing temperatures?

Yes!

Not really.

Yes!

No thanks!

ALCOHOL STOVE
(cheap and lightweight!)

ESBIT STOVE
(lightweight but more expensive than an alcohol stove)

LIQUID-FUEL STOVE
(great for extreme cold—also has a controlled flame)

CANISTER STOVE
(easiest to use and has a controlled flame for hiking in dry areas or high elevations)

I DID IT! DATE:

Always Cook Alfresco—in Open Air

Even if it is cold or windy, never cook inside your tent or other enclosed areas! The fumes given off by camp stoves can make you sick if inhaled in an enclosed setting. And of course always be prepared for possible burns from spilled food, fuel, and flames.

TAKE IT TO THE **NEXT LEVEL** ↗

Get Cooking

Once you have a camp stove, practice using it before you go into the backcountry. With the help of an adult, bring water to a boil and add oatmeal, grits, or a dehydrated meal. Then enjoy!

I DID IT! DATE:

CHAPTER 7

Water Treatment

If you go for a short day hike, you can fill your water bottle at your house and take it with you. But what if you are out on a multiday hike? Are you going to carry water for the entire trip? If you pass streams, springs, lakes, or rivers on your hike, you can get water along the way. But do you just dip your bottle in the water and drink it straight from the source? What if it looks crystal clear? Does that mean it is clean enough to drink?

Be aware: Water can be hazardous! One of the biggest threats is tiny bugs that you can't see without a microscope! These bugs make their way into the water through human or animal feces (a fancy word for poop), which means water sources near popular camping areas often pose a higher risk. Giardia, E. coli, and norovirus are just a few of the stomach "bugs" a hiker might get from drinking contaminated water. To lower this risk, always treat your water in the backcountry.

Right about now you might be thinking that you don't want to drink from natural water sources. But if treated properly, water from a cold mountain stream can be delightful and taste better than water from a faucet at home. And if you don't drink enough water, you will face another serious problem: dehydration.

Dehydration happens when your body doesn't have enough water to work properly. It can range from mild to severe. Signs of mild dehydration include feeling thirsty and having pee that is light to medium yellow. Symptoms of moderate to severe dehydration can include dark yellow or brown pee that smells super gross, red or flushed skin, and a parched or extremely dry throat and mouth. If severely, severely dehydrated, a hiker might lose the desire to drink, and the skin will shift from red and hot to pale, cool, and clammy. This means the person is entering a state of shock, an emergency situation that requires medical attention as soon as possible.

The good news is that dehydration can easily be prevented by drinking plenty of water and eating snacks. To protect against illness and dehydration in the backcountry, here are some ways to make clean, drinkable water:

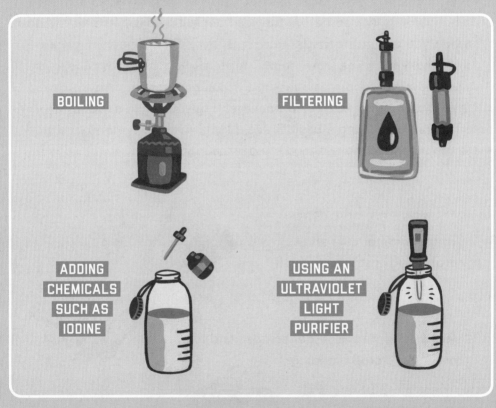

BOILING

FILTERING

ADDING CHEMICALS SUCH AS IODINE

USING AN ULTRAVIOLET LIGHT PURIFIER

These options are covered on pages 235–239. In the meantime, drink plenty of water on your hikes, but *only* collect it from the trail if you have the tools and knowledge to make it safe to drink.

CHAPTER 8

First Aid Kit and Toiletries

First Aid

First aid is exactly what is sounds like—the help given to someone who is sick or injured before they can get full medical attention. And when you are in the wilderness, it is incredibly important because you might be miles from help. The items you carry into the backcountry might help stop bleeding, stabilize a sprain, or even save a life. You won't be able to carry everything you might need for every situation, but having a basic first aid kit is invaluable. Here are some items that could be useful in the backcountry:

BANDAGES IN A VARIETY OF SIZES
To cover minor cuts and protect against infection.

GAUZE PADS AND ADHESIVE
To cover burns and larger scrapes and to apply pressure to stop bleeding.

ALCOHOL PADS
To disinfect wounds.

ANTIBIOTIC OINTMENT

To prevent infection in minor scrapes or cuts.

LIGHTWEIGHT SYRINGE

To flush wounds with clean water.

ASPIRIN OR IBUPROFEN

To treat pain, fever, and inflammation.

ANTIHISTAMINE (SUCH AS BENADRYL)

To treat allergic reactions.

MOLESKIN

To prevent blisters where friction might create hot spots on your skin.

ANTI-ITCH LOTION

To treat insect stings or topical reactions to plants.

TWEEZERS

To remove splinters and ticks.

NEEDLE OR SAFETY PIN

To help drain blisters.

ELASTIC BANDAGE

To prevent swelling of a sprain or immobilize an injured limb.

NONLATEX GLOVES

To prevent exposure to blood or other bodily fluids and prevent the spread of infection.

CPR POCKET FACE SHIELD

To give rescue breaths safely during CPR.

PAPER AND PENCIL

To jot down notes. Keeping track of symptoms is key to someone's care. If you can track changes over time, then you will be able to determine whether a hiker's condition is improving, declining, or staying consistent. Notes will also provide more information for a medical worker if necessary.

Do you need any medications? Do you have any allergies or asthma? List those items here:

....

....

....

TRY IT → Assemble a First Aid Kit

You can buy a preassembled first aid kit, but you can also put one together at home!

STEP 1 Find a waterproof bag to keep your first aid items in. It doesn't have to be anything fancy; you can use a ziplock bag. Use a permanent marker to label it first aid.

STEP 2 Gather the items from pages 52–54 that you already have in your home and put them in the bag.

STEP 3 Make a list of items you still need to get, buy them, and add them to the bag.

STEP 4 Every time you use something out of the first aid kit, replace or refill it.

STEP 5 Take your homemade first aid kit with you on your hikes and backpacking trips. Keep it in your car or pack so that you are always ready!

I DID IT! DATE:

Toiletries

Toiletries might not be quite as important as first aid, but they can improve the quality of your trip. You will not be as clean as you normally are—at home you have the luxury of a shower. But hygiene is just as important in the backcountry as it is at home. These items can be kept in something as simple as a ziplock bag.

TOOTHBRUSH A travel size will cut down on weight.

TOOTHPASTE Travel-size toothpaste is also easy to throw in your bag.

DENTAL FLOSS Floss is very lightweight and can double as string.

UNSCENTED HAND SANITIZER Get used to having dirt on your hands. But hand sanitizer is good to use after you go to the restroom in the woods. Speaking of . . .

TOILET PAPER If you are in the woods for any length of time, you'll need to go to the bathroom. You don't need to carry a whole roll or even the cardboard center. Pack three feet (one meter) of toilet paper per day per person and store it in a ziplock bag.

DEODORANT Some people carry a travel-size deodorant. Some people decide not to carry one at all because— let's be honest here—after a few days in the woods, whether you are wearing deodorant or not, you have that "hiker funk."

BANDANNA OR BABY WIPES If you camp near a stream, river, or lake, then you can rinse off at night with water and a bandanna. You shouldn't use soap—not even biodegradable soap—in or near backcountry water sources because it can negatively impact sensitive plants and animals. As an alternative to a sudsy soak, some people like to wipe themselves down with unscented baby wipes before getting into their sleeping bags at night and then simply pack out the wipes with the rest of their trash.

List any other items you need or want to be comfortable and feel clean in the backcountry, such as a hairbrush, nail clippers, or tissues.

TRY IT →

Assemble Your Toiletry Kit

Just like with your first aid kit, you probably already have most of the items you need.

STEP 1 Find a waterproof bag to keep your items in. Use a permanent marker to label it TOILETRIES.

STEP 2 Gather the items from pages 56–57 that you already have in your home.

STEP 3 Repackage the items in a way that makes sense for backpacking and pack them in your waterproof bag. You want things to be compact and light. For example, you probably don't need an entire package of baby wipes. Take out an appropriate amount and put them in a baggie.

STEP 4 Take your toiletries kit with you on backpacking trips. Or keep it in your car or pack so that you are always ready!

I DID IT! DATE:

TAKE IT TO THE NEXT LEVEL ↗

Be Ready to Help

Simply carrying first aid items is not enough. It is essential that you know how and when to use them. If you plan on spending time in the wilderness, look into some local CPR and first aid classes. Even better—take a class that is specific to the outdoors, like a wilderness first aid class. It just might save someone else's life— or yours.

I DID IT! DATE:

CHAPTER 9

The Ten Essentials (and the Important but Not-So-Essential Essentials)

There are certain items you should *always* take into the woods with you. They are key to saving your life in an emergency. Most people who trek into the backcountry carry these Ten Essentials:

1. SHELTER ▶ Some form of shelter is important if you get lost and unexpectedly need to spend a night outside, or if you encounter bad weather and need to hunker down.

2. NAVIGATION TOOL ▶ A compass and map or handheld GPS device can help you if you get lost. Or better yet . . . it might keep you from getting lost in the first place!

3. LIGHT SOURCE ▶ If you do get lost and your hike takes longer than planned, what would you want with you once it gets dark? A headlamp or flashlight.

4. FIRE STARTER ▶ What if it gets cold and you need to generate heat? You would need something to help you make a fire. Throwing in some matches or a lighter is a necessity.

5. FIRST AID SUPPLIES These are handy to treat anything from blisters to more serious injuries. See chapter 8 for what to include in a basic first aid kit.

6. REPAIR OR TOOL KIT A repair kit might include duct tape, a knife, or anything that can fix your gear out in the field.

7. SUN PROTECTION Sun protection is important on sunny *and* cloudy days. This could be sunscreen, sunglasses, a hat, lip balm, or clothing that will cover your skin.

8. EXTRA CLOTHES For those cold, wet, and windy days, the proper amount of insulation might include a jacket, gloves, and a hat. Higher elevations have colder weather, and it often sneaks up on you!

9. WATER What you put in your body is just as important as what you put on your body. Always take more water than you think you will need.

10. FOOD You need to fuel your body to go on the adventure in the first place. Like water, always take more food than you think you will need. You do not want to get stuck without food or water.

The Not-So-Essential Essentials

While you should always have the Ten Essentials in the woods, there are other items that are useful, if not 100 percent necessary. These items can make your hike easier, more comfortable and enjoyable, and give you peace of mind:

WHISTLE To signal for help in times of distress. Some people consider this an essential item.

CELL PHONE OR WATCH A smartphone can be a handy multi-tool on the trail that includes a clock, compass, and camera. If you don't pack a cell phone, consider bringing a watch so you can keep track of time.

TROWEL To dig a hole to bury your waste after going to the bathroom.

TREKKING POLES To reduce the impact on your joints and provide balance on tricky terrain or during river crossings.

PACK COVER OR GARBAGE BAG To protect your pack when it rains. Some people like to put a cover over their pack—it does not keep the backpack completely dry, but it helps. Others choose to line the inside of their backpack with a trash bag. The outside might get wet, but the items inside will remain dry.

RAIN GEAR To provide an additional layer of warmth and protection from the weather. Some people consider this essential.

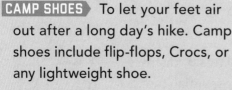

CAMP SHOES To let your feet air out after a long day's hike. Camp shoes include flip-flops, Crocs, or any lightweight shoe.

DUCT TAPE To fix gear, prevent blisters, or use in any other way you might think of. If duct tape is not a part of your repair kit, consider adding it or wrapping some around your trekking poles or another item so you have a bit on hand.

PAPER AND PENCIL To leave someone a note, record something on your map, or write down information if someone gets hurt. Pencils are a good choice because they don't run out of ink and you can sharpen them with a pocketknife.

HOLD IT TOGETHER!

If you know how to sew, a needle and thread is a great addition to your pack list. You never know when your shirt, jacket, pants, sleeping bag—just about any piece of gear—will get a tear. And if you don't know how to sew . . . duct tape to the rescue! Duct tape is a temporary fix, but it will usually hold for a while. Again, you don't know when you will have an emergency.

CHAPTER 10

Technology

In 1955 Grandma Gatewood hiked the Appalachian Trail with nothing more than an army blanket, a raincoat, a shower curtain as a tarp, and a small sack. She even wore Keds instead of fancy hiking shoes! But today you will find some pretty neat ways that hikers use technology—or you can simply choose to leave technology behind.

Satellite Navigation and Rescue

If you are worried about getting lost or lack confidence in your ability to read a map and use a compass, carry a Global Positioning System (GPS) for backup. A GPS is a satellite-based navigation system. A GPS designed for hiking typically uses easily replaceable batteries, is water resistant, and can connect to satellites even in remote areas. (You can read more about using a GPS device in chapter 17.)

A personal locator beacon uses satellites to send an SOS signal and your location to rescue agencies. A satellite messenger can send personal, nonemergency messages as well as an SOS and your location.

Cell Phones

Cell phones are pretty common now on trails. You can even get service on many ridgelines or summit peaks! They can certainly be a safety and rescue tool in some areas, but you can't rely on a cell phone as a rescue device because there is always a chance that you will have zero battery life or zero service.

Consider others around you before you use your cell phone to make a phone call or play music. Some people are in the woods to get away from the noise of a city or everyday life and to enjoy the sights and sounds of the nature around them.

Even if you never make a call, a smartphone can be a helpful multi-tool in the backcountry. Many people use the camera on a smartphone instead of carrying a larger camera. It is a great way to document your adventure because it will usually fit in your hip-belt pocket for quick and easy access. Sometimes there is an information board at the trailhead with maps and other important memos. Snap a picture of the map (although this should not replace an actual map) so you have a quick reference. Maybe there is a warning about an animal or a place listed where you can get water. Perhaps there is a list of local emergency numbers. Getting a picture of this information could be helpful down the trail.

Smartphones usually have built-in tools that can be useful on the trail. For example, there is usually a compass. They also have a place where you can jot down notes. The flashlight component might help if you get caught after dark and you forgot your headlamp. If you have cell service, you might be able to see if the weather forecast has changed. Most phones also have a health app already loaded.

It allows you to see how far you have walked, how many steps you've taken, and how many floors you've climbed. When you climb a tall mountain, you might find out you have climbed the equivalent of a landmark skyscraper!

There are also lots of cool apps that can enhance your hike. Are you interested in identifying leaves or wildflowers? There are apps for that! Maybe you are curious about a mountain peak off in the distance. You can even download an app that will show you the peaks you are looking at.

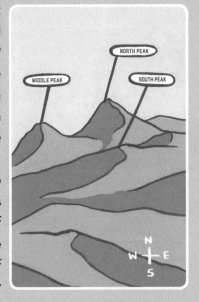

Of course, you will probably want to share your adventures with your friends and the world. But don't put number of "likes" ahead of safety. A good picture or video is never worth putting yourself at risk. When taking a picture, video, or selfie, keep these things in mind:

→ **Don't get too close to the edge of a cliff or drop-off. Always be aware of your surroundings.**

→ **Stay away from slippery rocks near fast-moving water. This includes rocks near or above a waterfall!**

→ **Respect the wildlife by giving them space. Wildlife is just that—*wild*! Wild animals behave unpredictably, and it is not worth putting yourself in harm's way. See page 284 for guidelines on staying safe around animals.**

Airplane Mode

If you are using your cell phone a lot and want the battery to last longer, put your phone in airplane mode. You will still be able to use the camera and most apps, but it will extend your battery life.

Keeping Your Cell Phone Alive

If you are in freezing temperatures, keep your cell phone close to your body. The battery will drain quickly if it is in cold temperatures for an extended amount of time. If you are on a backpacking trip, keep your cell phone with you in your sleeping bag at night.

There's an App for That

> **WHAT YOU'LL NEED**
>
> ➢ A computer, tablet, or phone;
> internet access; a pen; and paper.

STEP 1 What three things are you interested in learning more about on a hike?

1.

2.

3.

STEP 2 Search for an app that will help you learn more about each of your interests.

STEP 3 Check to see whether there's a cost to downloading the app. With a parent's permission, download the app and give it a try.

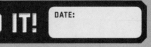 **I DID IT!** DATE:

SECTION 3

WHAT

TO

EAT

CHAPTER 11

Fueling Your Hike with Food

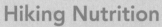

Hiking Nutrition

Food isn't just something to enjoy on the trail, it is a necessary piece of gear that will help you climb mountains and rack up miles. Calories are energy, food is fuel, and if you want to be a good hiker, then you need to have a good trail diet.

More is more when it comes to trail nutrition. Because you will burn more calories hiking than you do at home, you will need to eat more food. You will also probably need to eat more often. Hikers are well known for scheduling their meals a little like hobbits; they like to eat breakfast and then second breakfast, followed by lunch and second lunch. A lot of problems on the trail, whether it be fatigue and weakness or self-doubt and confusion, can be cured with food.

Because food is fuel on the trail, it is best to leave low-calorie and diet products at home in exchange for high-quality, high-calorie snacks. The more nutrients, fiber, and calories you can eat on the trail, the better you will feel. So if you want cereal in the morning, pack granola as opposed to Rice Krispies.

Sometimes it can be difficult to pack fresh produce because trail temperatures will cause the food to go bad quickly. And even if you have perfect conditions, there is a good chance that most produce will get smooshed and ruined in your backpack. A good strategy for getting fresh food on the trail is to take items that are less likely to bruise, like apples or carrots.

You can also take a wide selection of dried fruits and vegetables that you can eat by themselves or throw into meals to add taste and nutrition.

Nature's Refrigerator

One trick to help preserve produce and perishables longer on the trail is to put items such as sharp cheese into an airtight bag and stash it under a rock in a nearby creek while you camp. The cold water serves as a makeshift refrigerator on the trail!

Along with ample calories, hikers need fluids at regular intervals. Drinking enough water is just as important as eating enough food. Dehydration can sneak up on hikers without much warning, especially in the summer. It can cause them to feel sick and weak and lead to more dangerous conditions if left untreated. Luckily, most cases of mild and moderate dehydration can be reversed by steadily sipping on fluids and eating a few snacks.

Popular Trail Foods

One of the most magical parts of hiking and backpacking is that food almost always tastes better on the trail. You can pack a plain peanut butter sandwich, and after five miles of hiking, that ordinary nut spread smothered between two slices of bread tastes like a gourmet feast.

Perhaps this magic is due to hiker hunger or a lack of alternative food options, but there's no question that sitting by a waterfall makes food taste better. Whatever the reasons behind trail food tasting so delicious, there are certain foods that consistently claim the top spots as favorite backcountry snacks and meals.

Breakfast Ideas

→ Breakfast bars.

→ Make small bags of granolas loaded with extra raisins, coconut flakes, or chocolate chips and powdered milk, and add a little water.

→ Cook oatmeal with nuts, dried fruit, and brown sugar

→ Cook a pot of instant grits and add shredded cheese and bacon bits for flavor.

Lunch Ideas

→ Sharp cheese with crackers and jerky or cured meats such as sliced salami.

→ Peanut butter sandwich on bread, bagels, or tortillas. (Topping your nut butter with honey, chocolate spread, or raisins can help add variety.)

→ Tuna or chicken in a foil pouch with a small pack of mayonnaise and sun-dried tomatoes.

Dinner Ideas

→ Prepackaged dehydrated or freeze-dried dinners.

→ Mac and cheese.

→ Instant potoatoes or instant stuffing.

→ Ramen noodles.

→ Add water to dehydrated black beans or hummus and then consume their bean dip with corn chips and cheese.

Snack Ideas

→ Energy bars, nut bars, or candy bars.

→ Trail mix, dried fruit leathers, chips, and cookies or crackers.

→ Dark chocolate or instant warm pudding mix.

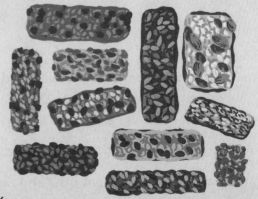

The No-Cook Method

Did you know that you can enjoy dehydrated and freeze-dried camp meals without carrying a stove? The traditional camp meals in a pouch come precooked, but the water is removed to make them lightweight and long-lasting. Usually hikers prepare these meals by adding boiling water to rehydrate the food and heat it up. However, you can also "cold soak" your dinner and have a meal that is filling and fully rehydrated, but not hot. You add the same amount of cold water to the pouch as you would hot water. The catch is that boiling water will have your meal ready to eat in fifteen minutes, whereas a cold soak will take a couple of hours. If you don't have a stove or want to save space in your pack by leaving it at home, a cold soak can deliver a filling meal without much hassle.

> **WHAT YOU'LL NEED**
>
> ⪢ A large ziplock bag, a measuring cup, and some of your favorite snacks, such as nuts, crackers, pretzels, dried fruit, and small amounts of candy or chocolate.

STEP 1 Measure out a cup of one of your favorite snacks. Pour the cup into a large ziplock bag.

STEP 2 Measure a cup of a different one of your favorite snacks, and add that to the bag as well.

STEP 3 Continue to add ingredients one cup at a time to the ziplock bag until it is half-full.

STEP 4 Zip the bag completely shut. Hold it with both hands and shake.

STEP 5 Pack your original, homemade trail mix on your next hike and share it with your family and friends.

I DID IT! DATE:

TRACK IT ↘

Your Favorite Trail Mix Recipe

Found the perfect combination of ingredients to fuel your adventures? Write the ingredients here so you never have subpar snacks again.

1 CUP EACH OF:

I DID IT! DATE:

 **Picnic on the Trail**

WHAT YOU'LL NEED

> A backpack, friends, and food for a picnic.

STEP 1 Make a meal plan for a picnic that you can share with friends and family on the trail. (If you can't get to a trail, feel free to host it in the backyard or a nearby park.)

STEP 2 Gather up your chosen goodies and pack them in your backpack.

STEP 3 Share a short hike with your friends until you find a spot suitable for a picnic. (Remember—better atmosphere means better-tasting food.)

STEP 4 As you unpack your bag of goodies, explain why you brought each item. Does it provide good energy? Is it packaged in a way that makes it easy to take hiking? Does it do well in any temperature?

STEP 5 After enjoying the picnic, ask your friends what they liked best about the meal. Would they bring anything else or do something differently? Some of the best trail recipes and meals are created when hikers combine ideas and food preferences.

 **I DID IT!** DATE:

Dry Your Own Fruit

Some hikers who get into food preparation and hiking nutrition will cook their own camping meals at home and then use a dehydrator and vacuum sealer to store them for their next backpacking trip. If you don't have a dehydrator, you can use a standard kitchen oven to make foods such as beef jerky or to dehydrate and preserve fruits like bananas, strawberries, apples, and pineapple.

Here's a recipe for making your own dehydrated banana slices:

STEP 1 Preheat the oven to 135 degrees.

STEP 2 Slice up several bananas. Try to keep the slices around 1/3 inch thick.

STEP 3 Line a baking tray with parchment paper and place the slices flat on top so that they are not touching one another.

STEP 4 Put the tray in the oven.

STEP 5 Rotate the tray every two hours.

STEP 6 Remove the tray after six hours and allow the banana slices to cool. Once they are cool, try a few pieces, and store the rest in an airtight bag in the freezer. Remember to grab them before heading out on your next hike!

I DID IT! DATE:

CHAPTER 12

Hiking and Backpacking Meal Planning

Deciding how much food to take with you into the backcountry is just as important as taking the right food. Creating a meal plan will help you stay fueled and happy on anything from a half-day hike to a weeklong backpacking trip. It's simple to do.

Create a chart for each day of the week that you will be on the trail and add a row for extra food. Include columns for snacks, breakfast, lunch, and dinner.

Next, fill in the chart with food items. Try to focus on foods that will make you feel energized and ready to hike. Based off your chart, make a grocery list of foods that you need to buy, then go shopping.

PEANUT BUTTER

APPLES

TORTILLAS

RAISINS

HARD-BOILED EGGS

PRECOOKED BACON

CHOCOLATE BAR

DRIED FRUIT

TRAIL MIX

GRANOLA BARS

DEHYDRATED PASTA DINNER

EXAMPLE DAY HIKE MEAL PLAN

BREAKFAST	SNACK	LUNCH	
breakfast at home before heading out	granola bar	bacon, lettuce, and tomato sandwich on whole wheat bread, dried fruit	

EXAMPLE MEAL PLAN FOR A TWO-DAY, ONE-NIGHT BACKPACKING TRIP

	BREAKFAST	SNACK	
Day 1	breakfast at home before heading out	trail mix	
Day 2	2 hard-boiled eggs, 3 strips of precooked bacon, dried fruit	trail mix	
Extra half day of food		trail mix, granola bar	

To make life really easy on the trail, cook or prepare any food that you can at home, such as hard-boiled eggs. (Also, because no one wants to put uncooked eggs in a backpack!)

You can also repackage your store-bought food to create proper portions for your trip, which will also help reduce bulk.

SNACK	DINNER	EXTRA SNACK
trail mix	dinner at home to relax and celebrate an awesome day	hard-boiled eggs and apple

LUNCH	SNACK	DINNER
peanut butter and raisins wrapped in a tortilla, apple	granola bar	dehydrated pasta dinner, half a chocolate bar
peanut butter and raisins wrapped in a tortilla, half a chocolate bar	granola bar	dinner at a restaurant to celebrate an awesome backpacking trip
1 tortilla, peanut butter		

And it doesn't hurt to double-check that you have everything from your list and in the correct quantities! Your stomach will thank you.

Writing down the food you want to eat is different from packing the right amount of it. You might want to eat oatmeal for breakfast, but don't put the whole family-size container into your backpack. Instead, look for single-serving packages or scoop a serving or two into a reusable bag that you can easily take with you on the trail.

When you create your meal plan, add one extra snack for a day hike and an additional half day's worth of food for a backpacking trip. Things don't always go as planned on the trail. You might get a sprained ankle and hike more slowly than expected, or you could be held up by a storm or linger at an awesome swimming hole. You don't want to carry a lot of extra food, but carrying a little extra will give you the flexibility to make good decisions on your hike.

Leftovers

When you go hiking and backpacking, you will have to carry all your leftover food in your pack. It's not a good or safe practice to bury, burn, or discard leftovers in the woods—especially if you don't want wild animals to come and look for your dinner scraps. So if you don't finish your mac and cheese at dinner, you'll need to scrape the ooey-gooey shells and cheese into a small trash bag and carry it with you. Packing the right amount of food can prevent you from carrying a sloppy bag of leftovers to the next trash receptacle.

While planning, you'll also have to decide whether or not you want to cook on the trail. Carrying a stove will influence what types of food you can write down on your meal plan. And if you do plan to take a stove, then you'll need to figure out how many meals you want to heat up as well as how much fuel that will require. Some hikers and backpackers like to cook just dinner; others will set up their stove for breakfast and dinner. If it is chilly or you like hot food, then you might want to cook three meals a day.

TRY IT → Carrying Your Food

WHAT YOU'LL NEED

➢ A backpack and a day's worth of food.

STEP 1 Gather all the food you plan to eat in one full day in your normal, everyday life at home.

STEP 2 Put all the food in your backpack. Does it fit? Is it heavy? Are you surprised by how much or how little food you packed?

STEP 3 For a full day, eat only the items in your backpack. This gets you used to carrying your food and only eating the items you brought with you.

STEP 4 At the end of the day, go through your backpack and evaluate how well you planned food for a day. Did you pack too much or too little? What would you do differently next time?

I DID IT! DATE:

TRACK IT ↘

MEAL PLAN FOR A THREE-DAY, TWO-NIGHT BACKPACKING TRIP

	BREAKFAST	SNACK	
Day 1			
Day 2			
Day 3			
Extra half day of food			

Make a meal plan for a three-day backpacking trip! Decide whether or not you will take a stove, and fill out your chart.

I DID IT! DATE:

	LUNCH	SNACK	DINNER

PART II

HIKING

You hit the trail with your day pack

full of snacks, water, a rain jacket, and a printed map of the nature preserve. After hiking two miles, you feel something wet against your back. Your water bottle is leaking, and there is a pool in your pack. Your gear is soaked and your map is blurry. It rips when you try to unfold it and figure out where you are amid a network of trails. But, the sun is shining bright and you are carrying a compass and a smartphone. Should you navigate back to the trailhead? Or should you press on? Either way, how are you going to get to where you want to go? What would you do?

SECTION 1

MAKING A HIKING STRATEGY

CHAPTER 13

Hiking Style

The first rule of hiking is HYOH—hike your own hike. There is no one right way to hike. You can go fast or slow. You can choose to take breaks or keep going. You may prefer to hike in a group and share conversation or lag behind and enjoy the silence. And while there might not be a single way to enjoy the trail, finding your personal hiking style and strategy can help you better enjoy your hike.

The best hikers are the ones who can apply different hiking styles and strategies when needed. You may not enjoy hiking fast, but if you are on a ridge and a storm is coming, then you can pick up the pace and descend to a lower elevation quickly. And if you never go slow, then you will probably miss out on observing and learning from the details and biodiversity along the trail. Here are some different techniques and considerations to keep in mind as you test out what you like most.

CHALLENGE HIKERS Challenge hikers strive to see how fast or how far they can travel and to test their physical limits. For those who enjoy an up-tempo pace, it is important to not let it lead to injury or directional errors. Hike hard uphill and be slightly more conservative and aware of your footing during the descent. Most hiking injuries happen on downhill slopes. And although it can be tempting to keep your eyes focused on the trail when cruising along, a fast hiker will also want to look up frequently to spot trail markers and upcoming junctions.

SLOW AND STEADY HIKERS The story of the tortoise and the hare, in which the slow and steady character carrying his shell outlasts his fast and furry competition, has been shared for over two thousand years for a reason. It is remarkable how much ground you can cover efficiently and effectively with a controlled and consistent pace as opposed to bursts of speed. If you take the slow and steady approach, then pack some extra snacks in your pockets. Hikers who stay within their ability level on the trail will need fewer and shorter breaks, so a lot of the eating and navigating can be done as you saunter down the trail.

STOP-AND-SMELL HIKERS Hiking isn't just about moving. While some hikers like to see how much terrain they can cover, others like to explore the terrain. The hikers who like to "stop and smell the roses" tend to take many breaks. They study flora and fauna, take pictures, or simply enjoy being still as much as or more than being on the go. Stop-and-smell hikers are usually happiest when they plan low-mileage outings and communicate their hiking style with any potential trail partners before they head out.

Hiking styles are personal, and they are all effective. Once you find your favorite style, though, it is still worth practicing and embracing other strategies. The ability to adapt can be extremely useful. For example, hiking fast and taking long breaks is great, until the trip where you feel a little under the weather and need to adopt a slow and steady pace to reach your destination. Or you may be in a group where you're not able to set the pace. If you can learn to embrace other styles, you won't feel pressure to compete with backpackers who charge past you, or lose patience with those who want to stop for a few hours in the afternoon to snack, nap, and journal.

 **Find Your Hiking Style**

> **WHAT YOU'LL NEED**
>
> ➤ A short trail or greenway near your house. (It's okay if you've hiked it before.)

STEP 1 Find a path near your home where you can hike by yourself or with a friend. Hike as naturally as possible. Go at whatever pace feels normal to you, and feel free to take breaks or plow ahead. If you are out there with a friend, hike in front to be sure that you are setting the pace. Describe your natural hiking style.

➤ What do you like about it?

➤ What do you dislike about it?

➤ Why do you think it feels normal to you?

STEP 2 Later in the day or on a separate occasion go to the same path and hike it as quickly as you can.

➤ How did it feel to hike as quickly as possible?

➤ Did you notice any shortness of breath or pain in your legs when you were pushing yourself?

➤ Did you feel proud or accomplished at the end?

STEP 3 Visit the same path a third time and go slowly, take breaks, and observe things in the surrounding environment that you may not have noticed before.

➤ What did you like about going slowly and taking breaks?

➤ Did you find anything surprising near the trail?

➤ Did you learn something new?

STEP 4 After you complete these three different hikes, ask yourself: "Which style do I want to use the next time I go hiking?"

I DID IT! DATE:

TAKE IT TO THE NEXT LEVEL ↗

Optimize Your Style

If you discover that you like going fast on the trail, then step it up a notch and try trail running or join a cross-country team. On the other hand, if you discover that you enjoy taking in your surroundings as much as moving through them, then check out some helpful field guides or apps that provide more details on your local environment. Or, you could do a little research to see if there is a local naturalist group, birding expedition, or mushrooming club that you can join.

I DID IT! DATE:

CHAPTER 14

Adapt to Your Environment

You are not in control of your environment—that's what makes going outside such an adventure! You will not be able to change the weather or the height of a mountain or how many bugs there are in the forest. You do, however, have choices when it comes to when you hike, where you hike, and how long you hike. And you can make changes to your hiking style and strategy that will help you on the trail.

Season

Maximize your favorite season by getting outside as much as possible. The different seasons bring different hiking conditions— if you usually lose feeling in your toes in freezing temperatures, then opt to hike more in the spring, summer, or fall. Or wait for a warmer winter day and venture out to lower elevations, where it won't be as chilly. On the other hand, if you can't stand bugs or snakes, then a snowy wonderland may be the perfect conditions for you to get outside. And expect the unexpected—a late-season snowstorm can hit in May or a sleet storm may ice a mountaintop you plan to climb in August. Other potential considerations include finding choice trails overrun with hikers during the most popular times of year or picking out a few fluorescent colors if you plan to head out during hunting season. But whether it is identifying spring wildflowers, chasing summer fireflies, watching birds fly south in the fall, or looking for animal tracks in the freshly fallen snow, there is something very special about hiking in each and every season.

Time of Day

You may not be a morning person, but if the temperature is going to be in the nineties during the afternoon, then drag yourself out early and cover some miles during the cooler part of the day. Picking the right time of day can optimize your hiking conditions. In many regions, hiking in the early morning will get you where you want to go before afternoon thunderstorms roll in. If it's cold or icy, then setting out later allows the sun to melt the ice off the rocks at your feet. However, if you are traveling over snow, you need to hike when it's not icy but before it's so warm that you sink to your knees with every step. If the route includes a river crossing, then hike it early in the day before it swells with additional snowmelt. Or, if you know a storm is coming through, then it might be worth pushing early and crossing the river before the rain comes.

Even when you don't have to account for extreme conditions, starting early in the day can still give you more flexibility with when and where you want to take your breaks on the trail, as well as how far you are able to go. You've heard the expression "The early bird gets the worm"? On a backpacking trip the early bird also usually hikes more miles or gets better campsites than hikers who start later in the day.

Terrain

You can't change the terrain of a hike, but picking the best route for your goals gives you the best conditions for your hike. If it has been raining for the past several days, then opt out of that riverside hike to a waterfall since the trail has a good chance of being muddy and sloppy or totally submerged under water. And if you know bad weather is coming in, you can keep to lower elevations with trees and limit your exposure. In the winter, instead of facing a winter storm with blinding snow and limited visibility on a ridgeline, watch the snow fall through the trees in an evergreen forest, which is also a pretty great place for a snowball fight if you are hiking with friends.

Night Hiking

How do you extend your miles and the time you have to hike each day? Start before the sun comes up or hike once it has gone down. Night hiking is a whole new way to appreciate the outdoors, and it only requires a headlamp and strong navigational skills. If you have never hiked in the dark before, then try it in the early morning hours before you do it at the end of the day. The advantage of starting at 4:00 a.m. is that you aren't tired from hiking all day, and in a few hours, the sun will be up to help you on your way. If you plan to do some night hiking, pack extra batteries or a backup flashlight and check your bearings frequently to stay on the right path. A GPS device or app is an extremely helpful piece of gear for staying on the trail during a night hike.

TRY IT → Night Hiking

WHAT YOU'LL NEED

➤ A headlamp or flashlight, a good map, a safe place to hike, and friends or family members.

STEP 1 Make a plan before setting out on your first night hike. Pick your team, pack extra snacks and clothes, and review the route you want to take.

STEP 2 Start hiking before the sun comes up. Do you notice how your eyes adjust to the light of the moon, the stars, and the rising sun? It typically takes less natural light than people think to make out the surroundings.

STEP 3 When you are hiking in the dark, use your headlamp or flashlight and stop every few minutes to make sure you are still on trail and heading in the right direction. Also, at some point, stop and turn off your light. Look up. Are there stars? What other things do you notice during your night hike that you couldn't have during the day?

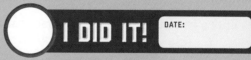

I DID IT! DATE:

TRACK IT ↘

Plan Go-To Hikes for Your Local Weather

What are the most common types of weather near you? Are there lots of wet months? How about extreme humidity and heat? Write three common weather forecasts where you live. What kind of hike will give you the most enjoyment in each kind of weather? For example, is the weather good for mountains views or do you want to stay lower or seek cover in the forest?

HIKE 1:

➤ The typical forecast usually calls for a high of .... degrees

and a low of .... degrees.

➤ There is usually a .... percent chance of rain or snow.

➤ The sun rises around .... a.m. and sets around .... p.m.

➤ Other conditions to consider (such as high winds, poor air

quality, or a full moon): ....

➤ Based on this weather, the best hike is: ....

....

➤ The typical forecast usually calls for a high of .... degrees

and a low of .... degrees.

➤ There is usually a .... percent chance of rain or snow.

➤ The sun rises around .... a.m. and sets around .... p.m.

➤ Other conditions to consider (such as high winds, poor air

quality, or a full moon): ....

➤ Based on this weather, the best hike is: ....

....

◖ HIKE 3: ▶

➤ The typical forecast usually calls for a high of .... degrees

and a low of .... degrees.

➤ There is usually a .... percent chance of rain or snow.

➤ The sun rises around .... a.m. and sets around .... p.m.

➤ Other conditions to consider (such as high winds, poor air

quality, or a full moon): ....

➤ Based on this weather, the best hike is: ....

....

I DID IT! DATE:

SECTION 2

NAVIGATION

CHAPTER 15

Basic Navigation

Early explorers used the sun's location and the length of shadows to guide their journeys during the day, and they relied on stars and constellations to point them in the right direction at night. If you are relying on the sky for direction, it can be difficult to follow a straight line during a storm. On the other hand, the sun and stars can't break or be forgotten at home, and they don't require batteries.

Finding North, South, East, and West

There are four cardinal directions: north, south, east, and west. If you can figure out one of the cardinal directions, you can determine the other three.

Every morning the sun will rise in the east, and every evening it will set in the west. If the sun is just coming up, you can point to it with your right hand and know that you are reaching that arm generally toward the east. Now stretch out your left hand in the opposite direction—that's west. With your right arm stretching to the east and your left arm stretching to the west, you're eyes will be looking north and your backpack will be facing south.

Finding Your Way at Night

Just because the sun goes down, you don't have to lose your sense of direction. It is possible to find north, south, east, and west at night, but first you will have to recognize two different star patterns. (Luckily, they look alike.)

One of the most well-known star formations in the Northern Hemisphere is the Big Dipper. It looks like a large soup ladle or ice cream scoop that is pointing up, away from the horizon. The two stars that create the far end of the scoop are known as Merak and Dubhe. If you draw an imaginary line starting at Merak and continuing up

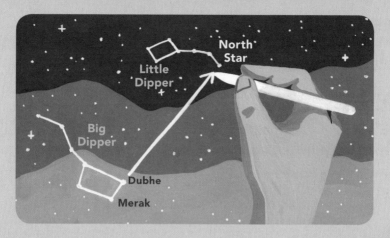

through Dubhe, you will hit Polaris, the North Star, which is the top of the handle of the Little Dipper. If you walk in the same direction of that line pointing toward the North Star, you will be hiking north. Keep it on your back if you need to head south. Let it rest on your right shoulder to hike west. And point your left shoulder toward it to head east.

Using Shadows

In the middle of the day, when the sun is directly overhead, it can be challenging to figure out which direction is east and which direction is west. However, if you stop for a while (this is a perfect moment for a snack) and watch the shadows move over a period of time, you can gain a general sense of direction. As time passes, the shadows will travel from west to east.

TRY IT → Find Your Direction

WHAT YOU'LL NEED

➢ A sunny day, two sticks, two rocks, and a clear space away from shadows. (A sandy or gravelly area will work best.)

STEP 1 Firmly place a stick upright in the ground.

STEP 2 See where the shadow of the stick lands and place a rock at the top of the shadow.

STEP 3 Wait fifteen to thirty minutes. (This is a great time to eat a snack or explore your surroundings.)

STEP 4 Shadows travel west to east. When you return to your stick, the shadow will have moved. Place the second rock at the top of the shadow in its new location.

STEP 5 Take your
extra stick and draw a
line between the two rocks.
Write a W for west near
the first rock and write an
E for east at the second rock.

STEP 6 Now put your heels on
that line between the two rocks.
Stretch your right arm to the east
and your left arm to the west.
Remember, when you line your
body up this way, you will be
facing north and looking away
from the south. Add the letters
N for north and S for south to
your hand-drawn compass!

I DID IT! DATE:

TRACK IT ↘

Map Your Backyard or Local Park

WHAT YOU'LL NEED

➤ A pen or pencil, a backyard or local park, and paper (optional).

STEP 1 Place this book or a sheet of paper flat on the ground or on a table.

STEP 2 Draw a vertical line. Label the top N and the bottom S. Cross it with a horizontal line and label the left W and the right E. This creates the map's compass rose.

STEP 3 Position yourself and the map so N points north. Draw a small X in the middle of the paper to represent the place you are standing.

STEP 4 Look around you. What are the most obvious permanent objects that you see? Maybe there is a large tree, a boulder, or a building? Draw the major features that surround you. If there is a large oak tree just to your left, then sketch it just to the left of the X. If there is a stream behind you, draw it south of the X. If you want to expand your map, walk to one of the major landmarks. Realign the north on your map with the direction north, and draw any new landmarks that you see in their appropriate locations.

Congratulations! You are now an official cartographer, a map maker!

I DID IT! DATE:

104

MY MAP OF:

Hide and Find Treasure

After you create a map of your
park or backyard, go back to the
place you mapped and hide some
"treasure" in a bush or under a
pile of rocks. If you're feeling
nice, it can be a special trail
snack, but if you're looking

to pull a prank on a sibling or friend, then maybe hide
something they use every day, like a favorite hair clip. Once
you mark where you hid the treasure in the appropriate
location on the map, hand it to a friend or family member. See
if they can read the map and find the treasure! (And prepare
for one of your everyday items to go missing very shortly!)

I DID IT! DATE:

CHAPTER 16

Map and Compass

How to Read Topographic Maps

Have you ever been on a hike and wondered when and where you would be at the highest point and potentially have the best view? A topographic map can help with that. A 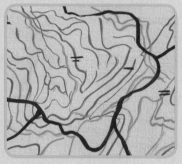 topographic map is flat, but it shows all three dimensions. These maps show the contours of the land and special features that help you determine where you are. Most topographic (or "topo") maps show landforms such as mountains, rivers, valleys, lakes, oceans, and roads.

A legend (also called a key) shows you what the symbols and colors that appear on the map mean. Streams, lakes, and rivers are often shown in blue. Green usually represents areas with thick vegetation and lighter areas are usually open terrain.

The scale of a map, usually found along the bottom, shows the distance on the map compared to the real-life distance. One map might represent many miles of land, so it certainly cannot be life size. Imagine trying to carry that on your hike! Cartographers provide us with a scale so we can figure out how far things really are from one another. For example, the scale might show that one inch is equal to one mile. So if you measure from one point to another and it is five inches on your map, it is actually a distance of five miles.

A topographic map shows the elevation of the terrain with wavy lines. These lines are called contour lines. Contour lines represent a change in elevation. So, the closer together the lines are, the steeper the terrain. Wide spaces between the lines mean the terrain is somewhat flat or has a gentle slope. Thicker index contour lines list their elevation so you can tell whether the elevation is increasing or decreasing between them.

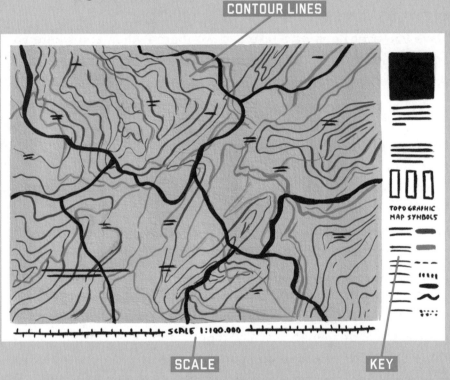

CONTOUR LINES

SCALE 1:100.000

TOPO GRAPHIC MAP SYMBOLS

SCALE

KEY

Topographic maps help you picture an area as it is in real life. Those squiggly shapes that encircle ever smaller squiggly shapes? They are mountains or hills. Valleys will be the spaces with few or no lines in between them. You can find ridges by looking for contour lines with decreasing elevation on each side. Lines bunched tightly together indicate cliffs. Out on the trail, practice matching the contour lines on your map to the terrain on your hike. Pretty soon you'll be able to look at a topo map and picture exactly what a certain route will involve and figure out where you are by the type of terrain you have passed.

Look at Your Map—a Lot!

If you keep your map in your backpack and never look at it until you are lost, it will be difficult to figure out where you are. The area where you end up won't always have features that are easy to identify. For example, when the world around you is covered in snow, all the peaks start to look alike. And maybe you can't see the trail down below because everything is white. But if you pull out your map at sharp turns, landmarks, or intersections and track your progress, you will be able to keep up with where you are and help yourself "stay found."

Getting to Know Your Compass

The earliest compass was a carved piece of naturally magnetic lodestone. As early as the fourth century BCE, the Chinese were known to use these "south pointers" to avoid getting lost. By the eleventh century CE, the Chinese had figured out how to magnetize needles and they were used for navigation on ships.

Today, magnetic compasses are still the best tool to find our way, and most smartphones even come with a basic compass app. When you are trying to reach a certain location, the terrain might not be flat and there might be obstacles in your way. By following the directions on your compass you are able to take short detours and still stay on track.

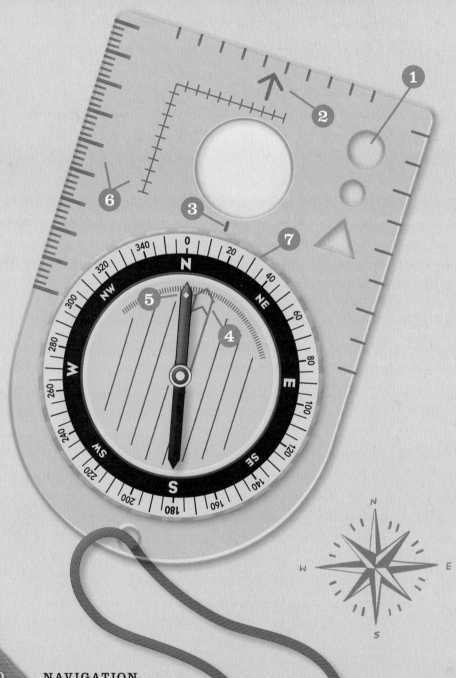

1. BASEPLATE It is clear so you can see through it to take bearings (the directions in degrees) from a map underneath.

2. DIRECTION OF TRAVEL ARROW It helps you maintain your path when you are following a bearing.

3. INDEX LINE OR BEARING MARKER Aligned with the direction of travel arrow, it indicates the bearing on the rotating bezel (see number 7 below).

4. ORIENTING ARROW It indicates where the magnetic needle should be positioned to follow a bearing.

5. MAGNETIC NEEDLE Usually painted red on its north end, it spins according to the earth's magnetic field and always points to magnetic north.

6. RULER It helps you figure out the actual distance using a map's scale.

7. ROTATING BEZEL Marked from 0 to 360, it converts cardinal directions into degrees.

How to Set Your Bearing

Not all hiking takes place on a dirt path. Sometimes you will walk over snow or sand or perhaps your hike will wander through open fields or plains. When you don't have a dirt path to guide the way, you will need to use the bearings on your compass to make sure that you are headed in the right direction. A bearing is simply a more precise way to describe a direction by using the degrees of a circle. So north is 0, east is 90 degrees, south is 180, and west is 270.

Let's say that you are out for a hike and the guidebook you are using reports that there is a historic cabin located a half mile off trail from the junction where you are standing. There is no trail leading to the cabin, so you will need to travel off the beaten path to find it. The guidebook provides a bearing of 135 degrees to reach the cabin.

If you want to travel 135 degrees (that is roughly southeast), then you will need to use a compass. It is important for you to keep the compass flat so the compass needle can correctly point to magnetic north. If you hold it straight up and down, the needle position may not be accurate. So, hold your compass in the palm of your hand at chest level and follow these steps to find the direction of the cabin.

1. Find 135 degrees on the rotating bezel and turn it so it aligns with the direction of travel arrow.

2. Turn your body until the compass needle is inside the orienting arrow. This is often called "putting red Fred in the shed."

3. Now look at the degree that the travel arrow is pointing to on the compass. If the travel arrow is pointing to 135, you are facing 135 degrees. Walk in the same direction as the direction of travel arrow while keeping red Fred in the shed, and in a half mile you should reach the historic cabin. But . . .

4. When you reach the cabin, you will also need to backtrack in the correct direction to return to the trail. If the cabin is located at 135 degrees southeast, you will need to walk the opposite direction to get back. What number is directly opposite of 135 degrees on the rotating bezel? (Correct answer: 315 degrees—roughly northwest.)

5. Repeat the first three steps using the bearing 315 degrees to get back to the trail.

Compass Fail!

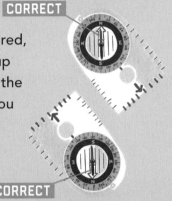

Before you start walking, make sure it is the red, north-pointing end of the needle that lines up with the orienting arrow. If the other side of the needle is aligned with the orienting arrow, you will end up walking in the opposite direction of where you want to go! Stop frequently and make sure you are still headed in the correct direction.

CORRECT

INCORRECT

North Versus North

True north is the geographic north pole, where all longitude lines meet. All maps show true north, usually at the top of the map. A compass needle, however, aligns itself with the earth's magnetic field, so it points to magnetic north, which is not the same as geographic north. The difference between magnetic north and true north is called declination, and it varies depending on where you are located. If you are practicing basic navigation concepts in your backyard, you will not need to account for declination as you become comfortable with your tools. However, when you take your map and compass skills into the backcountry and start traveling more than a few hundred yards, you will need to account for declination. Even being off by a single degree can cause you to miss your target by one hundred feet over a mile (forty-nine meters over a kilometer). That could be the difference between reaching an awesome viewpoint or stumbling into a mosquito-infested pond.

When it comes to finding your way out of the woods, getting "pretty close" isn't close enough. Learning to account for declination will help you reach your destination with precision. Different styles of compasses have different methods for adjusting the declination, so be sure to read through the instructions that come with your navigation tool to learn the best practices for your device. In every case you will need to find out the correct declination before you program or adjust the compass. The place to find the declination for your given location is the NOAA (National Oceanic and Atmospheric Administration) website. And if you take a family hiking adventure that is more than a few hours away—perhaps out of the state or even out of the country . . . Iceland here we come— then you will want to find the correct declination for that location and reprogram your compass.

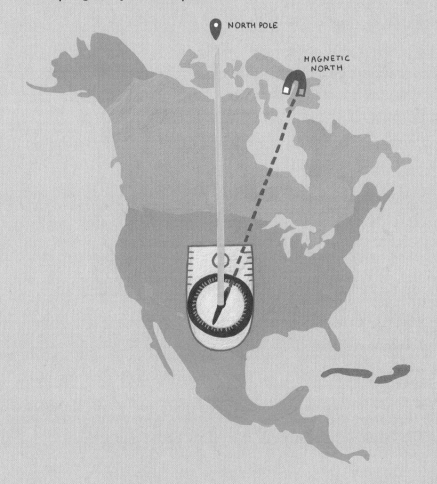

Use Your Compass

WHAT YOU'LL NEED

➢ A compass, a stick or rock, and space to walk around.

STEP 1 Mark your location with your stick or rock.

STEP 2 Set a bearing on your compass by turning the bezel so that the index line points to 0 degrees, or due north.

STEP 3 Turn your body until you have put red Fred in the shed (the magnetic needle in the orienting arrow).

STEP 4 Find a landmark straight ahead to help you stay in a straight line, and follow this bearing for exactly thirty paces and stop.

STEP 5 Set a bearing of 120 degrees on your compass and find another landmark.

STEP 6 Follow this bearing for another thirty paces and stop.

STEP 7 Set a bearing of 240 degrees and find your landmark.

STEP 8 Follow this bearing for thirty paces and stop.

Did you end up where you started? Are you close? Don't worry if you did not end up exactly on your marker. With a little practice, your navigation will become more precise. As you get better at this, you can increase the distance. Then it will be even more important for your bearings to be accurate.

I DID IT! DATE:

TRACK IT ↘ Follow in Your Footsteps

Use your compass to create a route in your backyard or a nearby park. Write down the bearings and how many steps "or paces" it is between each location. (You can walk between objects and landmarks if you want to make it easier to follow the instructions, but you don't have to.) After you zigzag to four or five different locations, hide a note or reward at the last stop. Retrace your steps one time to make sure your bearings and steps are correct. Now hand the information off to a friend and see if they can follow your tracks and discover the "treasure" at the end.

Here's an example of what your instructions might look like:

➤ Walk twenty steps at 75 degrees to an oak tree.

➤ From the oak tree, walk thirty-three steps at 150 degrees to a boulder.

➤ From the boulder, walk ten steps at 180 degrees to a park bench.

➤ From the park bench, walk fifty steps at 270 degrees to a lamppost.
Look for a note.

I DID IT! DATE:

Beeline Obstacle Courses

> **WHAT YOU'LL NEED**
>
> ➢ A compass and a friend. (You'll want to play this game outdoors in a green space such as a park or playground.)

STEP 1 Ask your friend to pick a bearing.

STEP 2 Find the bearing on your compass.

STEP 3 Walk 100 steps in the direction of the bearing while trying as hard as possible to walk in a straight line. That means you might have to climb over benches, under bushes, and through a game of kickball. The path might be relatively easy or it could be a challenging and hilarious obstacle course. It all depends on your environment and the bearing!

STEP 4 Now pick a bearing for your friend and watch their 100-step journey. As long as it is safe, be creative in going over, under, and through anything in your path to stay on a straight line.

I DID IT! DATE:

Navigate Your Map

Go to the map you made in chapter 15.
Use the landmarks on your map and
practice your compass skills.

➣ If you chose a tall tree and a large boulder,
   start at the tree.

➣ Turn the bezel on your compass the direction you want to
   walk (for example, from the tree to the boulder).

➣ Put red Fred in the shed and record your bearings. You
   can do this with multiple objects.

➣ If you are with a friend or parent, have them pick an object
   or landmark and tell you the bearing. See whether you can
   figure out which landmark they chose!

By practicing navigation, you will not only learn how to find
special off-trail locations, but you will also make sure that you
have the skills to stay found and not wander too far off course.
Once you start pinpointing your bearings and direction on a
compass and then counting your steps in any direction, you
should always be able to return to your starting point without
too much trouble.

I DID IT! DATE:

CHAPTER 17

GPS

On June 26, 1993, the US Air Force launched the twenty-fourth Navstar satellite into orbit. This completed a network of satellites known as the Global Positioning System. Now GPS is used in cars, on smartphones, in fitness trackers, on life-saving missions, in drones, and yes, even for hiking.

A GPS device can tell you where you are and track where you have been. Many people use some form of GPS to tell them which direction they need to go, whether in their cars or in the woods.

A GPS will show you where you are by giving you coordinates and your position on its map. It will also tell you your elevation and cumulative distance. A GPS uses tracks to show your path so you can look back at where you've come from. This is sort of like Hansel and Gretel leaving bread crumbs in the forest, but with technology.

How to Use a GPS on a Hike

Before you head out into the backcountry or on your next hike, enter the coordinates of your locations, or waypoints, into your GPS. You can also download an app such as AllTrails to find the waypoints for hikes near you. GPS will give you the distance and direction you need to go to reach your mark. Remember that a GPS will sometimes give you the distance "as the crow flies," as if you were walking in a straight line. More often than not, a trek through the woods will not take you in a straight line. If you are just using waypoints and trying to take the shortest route between locations, then expect to bushwhack or walk off trail to find your destination. On the other hand, downloading tracks from the trail you want to hike will help you stay on the path. If there is a track file or there are waypoints available for the route, you should be able to find them by searching reputable hiking URLs or a GPS app. Once you find what you are looking for, download it onto your GPS device. If there is not a track file for your hike, you can create one on your hike and share it online.

Prep for GPS Malfunction

Just like a smartphone, a GPS unit can be a valuable piece of gear—so don't bury it in the bottom of your pack! But technology should not be your only means of navigation. Take along your map and compass, too. Extreme temperatures can sometimes leave your GPS or phone inoperable, and too much moisture might leave your GPS or phone malfunctioning. In general, technology is not completely reliable. Batteries run out and devices fail. Clouds will not usually block satellite signals to your GPS, but sometimes thick trees, tall buildings, mountains, and tunnels can interfere.

GEOCACHING WITH A GPS

Geocaching is like a huge treasure hunt and has become a very popular outdoor activity! Geo means "earth" and cache means "a secure storage place." The caches usually hold little treasures and a logbook to sign. You might find a metal tin with stickers or painted rocks inside or a wooden box with special coins plus a notepad or pen (unfortunately, no candy, given bugs and animals). GPS devices are used to hide and find caches. The caches are placed at specific locations and marked by coordinates. The coordinates are posted on a website so others can find the containers. Then the "geocachers" use their GPS and sometimes a map to find the cache.

TRY IT → Record a Hike

WHAT YOU'LL NEED

➢ A GPS device or smartphone with a GPS app, and a friend or relative (optional).

STEP 1 Learn how to "record a track" on your specific GPS device.

STEP 2 Go outside and record a track as you wander around your backyard.

STEP 3 When you are finished, end the track recording.

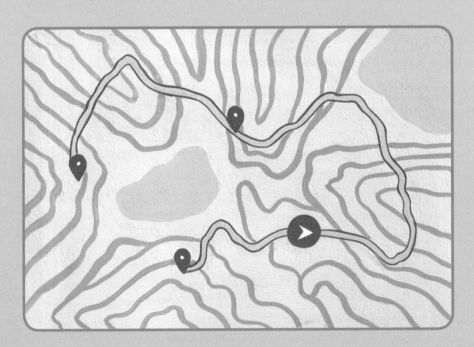

STEP 4 Hand the GPS device to a friend or relative to see whether they can retrace your route by following the track you made. Or, if no one is available to come outside, retrace the route backward by using the track you made.

I DID IT! DATE:

TRY IT → Find Caches

The next time you go for a hike, take along a smartphone with a geocaching app on it. Open the application and look for caches along your route. If you find one, sign the logbook, and if you take something from a cache, replace it with something else so the next geocacher also gets a treasure!

I DID IT! DATE:

 **TRY IT →** Find Your Latitude and Longitude

Finding the latitude and longitude of your house is pretty easy thanks to technology. If you have a smartphone or computer, there are websites where you can plug in your address and receive the coordinates. You can also use Google Maps to find the latitude and longitude of your home. Use one of these methods and record your findings below.

LATITUDE AND LONGITUDE COORDINATES

Can you think of another location you would like to find the GPS coordinates for? Repeat the process and record your findings.

LOCATION

COORDINATES

I DID IT! DATE:

Hide Your Own Geocache

You can also hide your own geocache in the woods. One idea is to collect several small rocks and paint cool designs on them. Then you can stick the rocks and a notepad and pen in an old metal lunch pail and hide it in the woods. Be sure to leave a note encouraging folks to take a painted rock and write their name, the date, and any notes inside the logbook. Record the location on the geocaching app. Then, the next time you hike that trail, check the logbook to see if anyone else visited your cache.

I DID IT!   DATE:

ENVIRONMENTAL EXTREMES

CHAPTER 18

Sun and Wind Exposure

Sun

If you have ever been to the beach or spent the day playing outside, you've probably had a sunburn. Even a red nose and pink cheeks are a sign that you've spent too much time out in the sun. Now imagine that you are living outside on the trail for a few days (or even more), possibly exposed to the sun all day. It would be easy to get a burn, but it's also not hard to avoid it.

The sun helps our bodies make vitamin D, which allows our bodies to absorb calcium and makes our bones stronger. But the negative results of the sun's rays can also hurt our bodies, causing chapped lips, a sunburn, skin damage, and even skin cancer. This doesn't mean you should stay inside all the time! But it does mean that you need to take precautions and protect your skin when you are exposed to the sun. Here are some options:

→ Slather up with sunscreen before heading out! Use a generous amount and reapply. Remember that you sweat as you hike, so it might come off quickly. Pay attention to areas like the tip of your nose and your ears, which are easy to forget but are getting sunlight most of the day.

→ Sunglasses seem like a fashion accessory, but when you spend time outside, they are important protection. So throw some literal shade on your eyes.

→ Regularly apply lip balm with an SPF (sun protection factor) to keep your lips from getting burned.

→ Wear a hat—especially a wide-brimmed hat—to shield your head and face from the sun. There are even hats that have pieces of cloth that cover your neck. You may think you are covered with a baseball cap, only to find out the back of your neck is bright red at the end of the day!

→ Wear lightweight pants and long-sleeve shirts to cover your entire body. Most people choose light colors so the sunlight reflects off the clothing instead of being absorbed by darker colors.

→ Sun sleeves are a lightweight option if you don't want to wear a long-sleeve shirt. They provide coverage for your arms and slide on and off easily. Similarly, sun gloves can protect your hands, which get a lot of sun exposure.

→ Carry an umbrella when you are hiking in areas of extreme sunlight, like the desert. When you are in the desert, there are often long stretches without trees or shade, so create your own! There are lightweight umbrella options that are much easier to carry than the ones we use in a rainstorm.

→ Limit sun exposure between the hours of 10:00 a.m. and 4:00 p.m. This is when the sun's rays are the strongest. If you are hiking during these hours, take long breaks in the shade. Use shade from trees-or from an umbrella or a tarp if you need to.

Do you know that a sunburn is actually a first-degree burn? It's the same as when you accidentally burn your finger on a hot pan.

But if a sunburn is bad enough that it blisters, it might have reached the second-degree burn stage. Visit a doctor or urgent care medical center for professional help and medication. You can also read more in chapter 50.

Sunburn on a Cloudy Day

Just because you don't feel the sun doesn't mean you can't get a sunburn. Some people think you can't get burned on a cloudy day, but that is not true! When you climb to higher elevations, especially above the tree line, the air often feels cooler and may be breezier. But you are now exposed to more intense light because the sun's rays have less atmosphere to travel through. Burns at high elevations can happen faster than at lower elevations.

Wind

Sometimes you will have pink cheeks at the end of a day spent outdoors. It's odd because you used lots of sunblock, and it wasn't even sunny out. In fact, it was blustery!

Windy conditions, especially for long periods of time, can take a physical toll on your body. Wind can make climbing more difficult and cold days colder, and leave you with chapped skin. If it is gusty enough, it might even knock you down! When you are fighting the wind, it might be difficult to stop and read a map, drink water, and eat. You will need to find a sheltered area where you can take a break and do these things. If you don't, you might find yourself lost, dehydrated, and weak—and still dealing with the wind.

Taking care of yourself in the wind includes protecting your eyes, especially in sandy areas. It's a good thing you brought those sunglasses along! And just like with sun exposure, if the high winds last long enough, seek shelter to give your body a break from it. If the wind speeds are high, or if the windchill (the temperature it feels like with the wind) is low, consider adjusting your route to avoid exposed areas. Ridgelines and bare summits in the mountains are often dangerous places to be because they are not protected.

Extreme Wind

Mount Washington, New Hampshire, holds the second-highest recorded wind speed on the earth's surface. The mountain's weather is so extreme that wooden buildings on the top of the mountain have to be chained down. The record-setting gust clocked in at 231 miles per hour (372 kilometers per hour)! A Category 5 hurricane has wind speeds of at least 157 miles per hour (253 kilometers per hour), and it causes catastrophic damage. Imagine what wind at 231 miles per hour would do! You can hike up to the summit of Mount Washington, but check the weather forecast and know that it can change extremely fast!

TRY IT →

Create Your Own Shade

WHAT YOU'LL NEED

➢ Sunscreen, a hat, appropriate clothing for sun protection, water, and hiking gear.

STEP 1 Apply sunscreen and put on your sun protection layers. While you're at it, have a sip of water.

STEP 2 Spend some time outside. It can be walking, hiking, or even playing in your yard. Try to choose a time that isn't in the heat of the day.

STEP 3 Consider what you would do if there was no shade. Look around for something else that might work. Did you bring anything with you that might help?

STEP 4 Create a shady spot by using your hiking gear and the natural resources that surround you. Use branches, limbs, and leaves that have fallen on the ground, but don't pull or break any living plants for this practice exercise— only in case of an actual emergency.

STEP 5 Write down what you used or what you want to bring with you next time to help create your own shade.

I DID IT! DATE:

Do a No-Shade Hike

Plan and execute a hike where there is very little shade.

➢ Write a list of the items you need to take and wear to protect yourself from sun exposure.

➢ Make sure your entire body can be covered if needed. That includes your eyes, ears, and nose!

Also, jump ahead to chapter 21 to get more information on hiking through long waterless stretches.

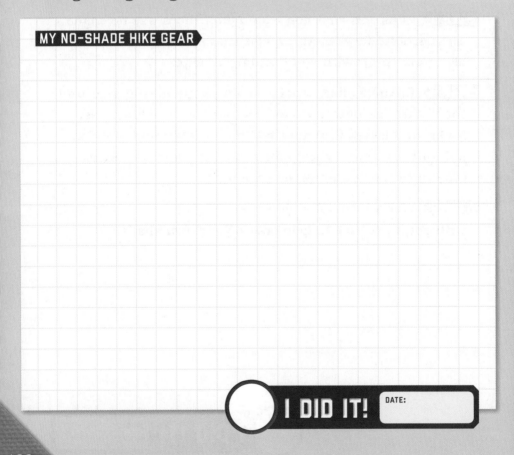

MY NO-SHADE HIKE GEAR

I DID IT! DATE:

CHAPTER 19

Snow and Ice

The world is a sight to behold when it is covered in white—and hiking is one of the best ways to experience it! But before you head out on a winter hike, check the forecast. Just because it's sunny and dry at the trailhead parking lot at 1,300 feet doesn't mean you can expect the same conditions a few thousand feet higher.

If there is a chance that you might encounter snow, take snow gear. It is always better to carry a few extra pounds of tools and not have to use them than to desperately need something you left behind. Here are a few options of what to add to your pack if you will be hiking in snow or on ice:

TREKKING POLES To give you more points of stability on the ground and help you balance. They are helpful when you aren't sure what is underneath the snow.

MICROSPIKES To provide extra traction under the sole of your shoe when you are hiking on hard-packed snow or ice. They usually have rubber frames that slide over hiking boots or trail runners and chains on the bottom that connect the spikes. They work best on fairly level terrain.

CRAMPONS To provide even greater traction under your shoes, especially on slopes and in more extreme conditions. Crampons have bigger spikes and you wear them to climb a slope, for ice climbing, or for mountaineering, which is a form of hiking that involves high elevation trekking and summiting mountains. Mountaineering requires more climbing skills than a typical walk in the woods.

ICE AXE To maintain balance when ascending or descending steep slopes. They can also be used to self-arrest—a fancy way of saying to stop yourself—if you slip and fall down a snowy slope. An ice axe is a technical tool and can be very dangerous if not used properly. The tip can pierce through skin, so handle it with extreme care and pack it safely on the back of a backpack when not in use. Never secure it in a way that could injure you in a fall. Never take an ice axe into the backcountry without understanding the parts of the tool and having some training in how to use it.

Imagine being on a trail, miles from civilization. Help is hours away at best, and it is easy to slip and fall on ice. So if you suddenly find yourself out of your comfort zone or in conditions that you don't have the correct gear for, the best decision is to turn around, no matter how bad you want to reach the summit, see that amazing view, or reach your mileage goal. You can return to complete the hike on a day with more favorable conditions.

When you are at higher elevations, expect that snow can fall any month of the year. Always carry layers, a sufficient sleeping bag, and shelter, because snow can begin unexpectedly and accumulate very quickly to create whiteout conditions, when snow limits your visibility—sometimes you can't see more than a couple of feet in front of you. When the sky is gray, the snow is falling, and the ground also turns white, everything blends together. This is very disorienting, and even on a familiar trail, it is easy to lose your way. If you don't know where you are or can't see the trail in front of you, it is better to set up shelter and get warm than to risk getting lost and becoming hypothermic. Once the snow has let up and visibility has returned, then assess the situation.

SUNGLASSES

Of course, sunglasses protect your eyes from the sun, but they are just as important in the snow. Snow blindness occurs if you are hiking at high altitudes, where the sun reflects off the snow or ice. Sometimes you won't even notice the glare until you already have some symptoms—pain, burning, and blurry vision. So take your sunglasses no matter what the weather!

Guesstimating Temperatures at Different Altitudes

You are planning a hike to a mountain summit, and the trailhead elevation is 1,000 feet. The temperature at the trailhead is 55 degrees Fahrenheit. The summit is at 5,000 feet. Knowing that the temperature might drop 3–5 degrees every 1,000 feet, what should you expect the approximate temperature to be at the summit? (If you would like to do this activity in metric, the general rule of thumb is that the temperature might drop 1.2 degrees Celsius per 100 meters.)

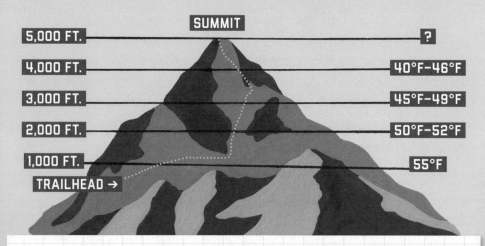

SUMMIT

5,000 FT.	**?**
4,000 FT.	**40°F–46°F**
3,000 FT.	**45°F–49°F**
2,000 FT.	**50°F–52°F**
1,000 FT.	**55°F**

TRAILHEAD →

Correct answer: 35°F–43°F

I DID IT! DATE:

Practicing a Self-Arrest—Without an Ice Axe

Did you ever lie on your side and roll down a hill when you were a young kid? Well, here's your chance to relive that experience and incorporate some winter mountaineering skills.

When a hiker slips on an icy or snowy slope, it is important that they stop themselves from sliding into jagged rocks or trees. With an ice axe in hand, a hiker will plunge the axe's pick into the snow or ice to suspend their fall. This is known as a self-arrest. An important part of this technique is having some type of body awareness while you are quickly sliding downhill.

You can practice responding to falls and become more aware of your body in motion by rolling down a hill (definitely more fun if friends are around to laugh along with you). But here's the catch: Once you pick up some speed, try to stop your body before reaching the base of the hill. Dig your hands and feet into the ground. Would gloves or other types of clothing help to add friction? Could you grab on to something?

This game is a great first step to learning how to control a fall on ice or snow!

I DID IT! DATE:

CHAPTER 20

River Crossings

Hopefully you've cooled off your feet in a refreshing stream of rushing water on a hot summer day. Spending a few hours by a river can mean a good foot soak, a rock-skipping competition, or a salamander search. Even better—perhaps you have pitched your tent next to a babbling brook and the sound was like a lullaby as you fell asleep. At some point, however, you might need to cross that moving water, and it could be nothing like a gentle lullaby. Sometimes you can rock hop or wade across a shallow and slow-moving stream or river. But other times the trail leads you to a raging river and continues on the other side of the water. If you get an uneasy (or maybe even terrified) feeling in your gut, pay attention to that feeling! Never head into any water before stopping to evaluate the situation. Water can sweep you off your feet (and *not* in a romantic way).

Where to Cross

Sometimes where a trail stops at the water is not the best place to cross. If the water looks dangerous, walk along the banks and find a more suitable crossing. Also look downstream and see what is there. If there are rapids or white ripples on the water, fallen trees, a waterfall, or other hazards, do not cross upstream of them.

If you slip and fall and are carried downstream, you'll head directly toward those hazards.

Paddlers will label a river from Class I to Class VI depending on how difficult it is to navigate. These classifications can also help you read a river and decide whether or not it is safe to cross. Only ford a river if you know how to swim and are traveling with a group. Do not try to ford a river that is higher than waist deep.

WHITEWATER RIVER RATING SYSTEM

CLASS I Flowing water with small waves and very few obstacles.

CLASS II The waves of water are a little stronger and bigger, perhaps with white crests.

CLASS III The waves are bigger yet and hard to predict. You can see the water change direction due to a strong current or occasional eddy. Cross with extreme caution.

CLASS IV Bumpy, big waves and turbulent conditions. Definitely not a good place for a swim—or a ford.

CLASS V This is when the river becomes a roller coaster. Only expert boaters will try to paddle Class V rapids. Hikers should safely take pictures from the shore.

CLASS VI A dangerous combination of waterfalls, powerful currents, and huge waves. Eek! Absolutely do not cross.

You might think the best place to cross a river is where it is the most narrow. But that is often where the water is flowing the fastest because it is all being funneled into a tiny area. Often, the widest part of the river will be the safest bet. The water will usually be slower in the wider areas. Sometimes there will be an island in the middle of the water, which causes the water to split into two directions. This is known as a fork; multiple splits are a braid. This is an even better option for crossing because the force of the water is divided.

FORK

BRAID

Another option, if the water is low enough, is to rock hop. If the jump between two rocks is far apart and there is a chance of slipping into a dangerous current, the rock hop is not a good option. You also might be able to walk or scoot your butt across a fallen log. But check a few things first: How high above the water is the log? If you fall, could the water pin you under the tree? Make sure the log is secure. If the log is wet or a fall means that you land on rocks, do not attempt it. You could put yourself in an even more dangerous situation!

How to Read a River

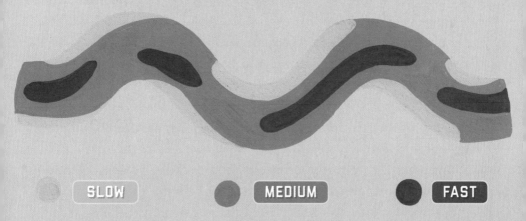

SLOW   MEDIUM   FAST

Slippery When Wet

Warning! Wet logs and rocks are very slippery! Carefully assess how slippery they are before using either as a means to cross a swollen river.

GOOD LOG

LOW   SECURE   DRY

ABOVE WATER

BAD LOG

NOT SECURE

VERY HIGH   WET

ABOVE ROCKS

How to Cross

Once you make the decision to cross, address your footwear. You will be walking on slippery rocks as you make your way across. You do not want to do this barefoot! You run the risk of slipping, getting your foot caught, or cutting your foot on something. Wear your shoes and socks for the crossing, or wear your shoes, but take your socks off and pull the insoles out of your shoes. That way, when you get to the other side and put them back on, it won't take as long for your feet and shoes to dry.

The best place to put your insoles and socks is inside your pack where they can't fall out. You do not want to be in the backcountry without appropriate footwear. Don't risk losing your balance trying to catch a sock that is floating downstream. This would also be a good time to secure any loose items that are hanging off your pack.

And make sure any electronics, your sleeping clothes, and sleeping bag are in a waterproof bag.

Trekking poles can help you make your way through the water and across slippery rocks. They give you another point of contact with the ground. Keep your feet planted and move your trekking poles to a secure place before lifting your feet again. If the current is strong, slightly angle your body upstream and step sideways. Take small steps and don't lift your second foot until the first one is secure.

If you are with friends, use a group technique. Groups of three can form a triangle by holding on to one another's waists.

Moving together through the water makes you a stronger force against the water. If you have more than three people, form a line or circle by holding on to one another's arms or waists. This way everyone supports everyone else. These techniques require a lot of communication and teamwork. A strong hiker with good leadership skills should lead the group across the water, calmly and loudly calling out steps in order to keep the group in sync.

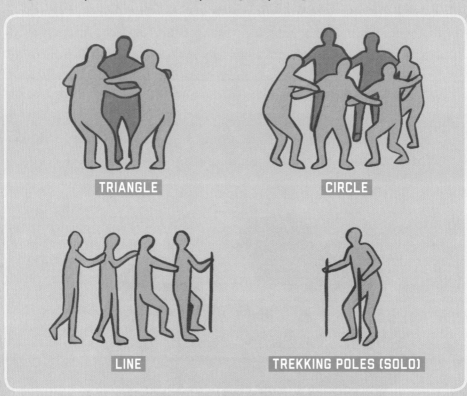

TRIANGLE

CIRCLE

LINE

TREKKING POLES (SOLO)

Okay, You Fell in the Water—Now What?

So what do you do if you fall during a river crossing? If the water is mellow, hopefully you are just a little wet! But if you get swept downstream and your backpack is waterlogged and holding you under, get rid of your gear! At this point, it is better to save yourself than your stuff! If your backpack is only destabilizing you, you can also just unbuckle the sternum straps but keep the hipbelt buckled so your pack can't pull you under. Either way, be prepared to ditch it in an emergency.

After you have your backpack off, float on your back with your feet facing downstream. Look downstream and use your feet to keep yourself from crashing into rocks and other obstacles. Look for the fastest way possible to get out of the current and use your arms to help you swim to shore.

Once you are on land, though, you are not out of danger. You are possibly cold, wet, and without your food, dry clothes, and gear— but you are alive and can use your brain and wilderness skills to see yourself out of this situation. There are tips on page 408 that can help you stay safe and more comfortable in such a situation.

Out and Back

Is this an out-and-back hike, where you return to the trailhead on the same route you took to your destination? If the river crossing seems tough now, think again before you cross. There is a chance that the water might continue to rise and be even more difficult when you hike back. Also look at your map. Is this your only water crossing, or do you have more ahead of you? If you have multiple crossings, turning around could be the best option. Don't get trapped in the woods because you are unable to ford a dangerous river.

If you do get trapped, the best plan is to wait for water levels to drop. Heavy rainfall or snowmelt will often cause streams and rivers to rise. When the water levels are too dangerous to cross, wait for a few hours, or even pitch your tent and assess the situation the next morning. If the rain has stopped, or the snowmelt refroze overnight, chances are that the water will be lower in the morning. If it is still too dangerous, it is time to come up with a new plan. Hike upstream to find a place to safely cross where the water is moving more slowly. Postponing a river crossing, or even turning around, is a much better option than fording through risky water.

River Crossing Techniques

Gather some friends and try out some river crossing techniques before you are in the water!

WHAT YOU'LL NEED

➤ A couple of friends, and any objects that can be used as obstacles.

STEP 1 Find an open area that can be your "river crossing," and place the obstacles on the ground.

STEP 2 Decide on a technique—triangle, line, or circle.

STEP 3 Choose a team leader.

STEP 4 Try to make it across your "river" without hitting any obstacles. Your team leader will call out when to step and which direction. Never let the group break apart. If you let go in the middle of a real river, someone could be swept away.

I DID IT! DATE:

TAKE IT TO THE NEXT LEVEL ↗

Swiftwater Rescue

If you plan on backpacking in remote areas or places with a lot of snowmelt and high river crossings, consider taking a swiftwater rescue course. This class will teach you the proper ways to handle emergency scenarios that involve water, such as how to read a river, recognize risks, and stay safe. You will also learn techniques to rescue yourself as well as others in the water.

I DID IT! DATE:

CHAPTER 21

Waterless Stretches

Most people don't think about how much water weighs. We fill our glasses; enjoy our nice, cold beverage; and refill when we get thirsty again. We only start to pay attention to how much water weighs when we have to carry it over long distances.

So . . . how much does water weigh? One liter equals 2.2 pounds (1 kilogram).

Water is *heavy*! On average, people drink about one liter every two hours while hiking. How many miles do you hike in two hours? Maybe four miles? Let's say you are going on an eight-mile hike and your personal pace is two miles per hour. If you divide your hike by your personal pace, that would be about a four-hour hike. That means you need approximately two liters, or 4.4 pounds (2 kilograms), of water. If it is a hot day, maybe you need even more.

As a general rule of thumb, plan to take half a liter of water for each hour you are on the trail:

> **0.5 liters of water** x **the hours of the hike** = **the liters of water you will need**
>
> So, for example:
>
> → For a three-hour hike: 0.5 × 3 = **1.5** liters of water
>
> → For a five-hour hike: 0.5 × 5 = **2.5** liters of water
>
> → For a nine-hour hike: 0.5 × 9 = **4.5** liters of water

If you hike in an area where you come across water sources quite frequently, you can get away with carrying less water and filling up more often. (Don't forget to purify it! See chapter 7.) But in certain locations or in hot, dry seasons, you won't have that luxury. Most hikers carry water bladders, canteens, or plastic bottles full of water, so let's take a look at just how heavy that can get.

HOW MUCH DOES WATER WEIGH?

1 liter   **2.2 pounds (1 kilogram)**   roughly the weight of a cantaloupe

2 liters   **4.4 pounds (2 kilograms)**   roughly the weight of a toaster

3 liters   **6.6 pounds (3 kilograms)**   roughly the weight of a brick

 =  =

4 liters   **8.8 pounds (4 kilograms)**   roughly the weight of a gallon of milk

 = =

5 liters   **11 pounds (5 kilograms)**   roughly the weight of a cat

 = =

6 liters   **13.2 pounds (6 kilograms)**   roughly the weight of two bricks

 =  =

7 liters   **15.4 pounds (7 kilograms)**   roughly the weight of a large bowling ball

If you are cooking dinner with a stove, you'll either need to camp near a water source or include the extra water needed to prepare your meal.

If you are hiking in the desert, or a dry area, you run the risk of water sources being dry. Plan ahead and find out whether the water is flowing. Some springs and creeks are seasonal, meaning they only have water after periods of rain or snowmelt. Seasonal water sources are usually noted as such in a guidebook, but they are *not* usually marked on maps. If it hasn't rained recently or if you plan to hike in the summer or fall, then don't rely on seasonal water sources.

Inevitably, you will have to carry water where sources are few and far between. Here are a few tips to get through those long waterless stretches:

→ Hike during the cooler parts of the day—early in the morning and in the evening. Sit out the hottest part of the day in the shade, if you can. See page 131 for tips on making shade.

→ Camel up! Camels drink large amounts of water at one time. Get hydrated before you enter the dry stretch. Make sure you have had plenty to drink *before* you head off with multiple liters of water. Then, when you reach a water source, take some time to not just refill your water bottles, but also to rehydrate.

→ If you are carrying significantly more weight because of a heavy water load, you won't hike as fast. That means you'll need to plan for more time on trail, which means carrying even more water.

→ If you plan on cooking, use your stove while you are at the water source. That way you don't have to carry extra water just for cooking.

→ Carry a lightweight scarf or a bandanna, and soak it in any water sources you pass. Then, put it around your neck. This will help cool you off for a bit.

→ Wear a hat and other protective clothing. Make your own shade. Some people like to carry light hiking umbrellas to protect themselves from the sun when hiking in open areas with direct sunlight.

→ Know the signs of dehydration—see page 405. Take action before you feel so bad that you can't help yourself.

Water Weight

If you are carrying multiple liters of water, your pack may need some adjusting to fit right. Try packing the water in different places until the pack feels balanced. Keep some bottles in the side pockets and some inside your pack. As you drink the water, repack so the water weight is even.

WATER CACHES

Sometimes people leave water for hikers on long waterless stretches of trail. Never rely on these water caches unless you can confirm that they are full. Sometimes the cache runs out, so always carry more water than you think you need. If you get lost, injured, or delayed, you'll only have what you are carrying to get you out of the woods or desert. When you are hot and thirsty and in the middle of a dry stretch, water is liquid gold!

TRY IT → Hunt for Water

Next time you are in a dry area, test out your ability to find water when it seems like there isn't any. Of course, don't forget to bring your own water. This is just practice!

Some things to try:

1. Pay attention to areas with animals. After all, they need water, too! Mosquitoes, birds, and animal tracks could mean there is water nearby.

2. Look for green! If you see dense vegetation, there is likely a water source around.

3. Look for shaded areas that stay cool throughout the day. Rain, ice, and snow might last longer in these areas.

4. If none of these strategies work, get to higher ground where you can have a bird's-eye view and hopefully spot water or areas mentioned above.

◯ **I DID IT!** DATE:

Watering Up for Dry Stretches

Research a hike in a dry area or even the desert.

➤ Calculate the miles between water sources. Use your personal hiking pace to figure out how much time it would take to reach each source.

➤ How many liters of water would you need to carry between water sources?

For example, if you hike about two miles per hour and you are planning a twelve-mile hike where there is a creek after four miles, then you will need to carry two hours' worth of water (0.5 liters × 2) and pick up another four hours' worth of water (0.5 liters × 4) at the creek to finish the hike. That means you'll have to pack a few empty bottles as well.

I DID IT! DATE:

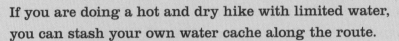

Make a Water Cache

If you are doing a hot and dry hike with limited water, you can stash your own water cache along the route.

WHAT YOU'LL NEED

➢ A gallon of water (or more), a map, and a compass.

STEP 1 Find the best access point to leave a water cache on your hike. Look at the map and study the route you plan to take. Does the trail cross any roads where you can easily drop off your water? Or are there any short side trails that quickly lead to an alternate trailhead? Try to pinpoint a location with easy access that isn't too close to the start or end point of your hike.

STEP 2 Cache the water. A day or two before your hike, travel to the water cache location and secure your water in a safe and hidden location. Mark on your map where you left the water cache, along with any notes or a description that might help you find it.

STEP 3 Enjoy your hike—and your water cache! On the day of your hike, use your map to travel to the site of your water cache. Isn't it amazing to enjoy all that extra water without carrying extra weight the entire way?! Be sure to pack out any bottles that you used to cache your water.

I DID IT! DATE:

CHAPTER 22

Lightning and Thunder

Have you ever seen a bright flash outside your window and then heard a loud *boom* shortly after? It can make you jump even when you are inside. Now imagine standing on the top of a mountain, the dark sky all around you, with no roof over your head. Lightning is unpredictable, and it can travel a long distance. If you hear thunder, you are already at risk of being struck by lightning.

Of course the best thing to do when it comes to lightning is to avoid getting caught in a bad situation to begin with. If you are at home and the weather forecast calls for storms for that day, postpone your hike. But if you are in the middle of a multiday hike, or if unpredictable weather rolls in, you can lessen your risk by avoiding exposed areas when thunderstorms are likely. On a mountain, for example, it's a good idea to reach the top by 10:00 a.m. and get back down by noon. Out on the trail, keep an eye on the sky. Tall white clouds that grow vertically with hard edges can be the first sign of a developing thunderstorm. If you are trying to make a quick decision in a lightning storm, remember this bit of advice: You should not be the tallest object in an open area. You also do not want to be standing next to the tallest object.

Know before you head out where the safest locations are and how long it will take to get to one.

You definitely do *not* want to be any of these places:

→ In open areas where you are the tallest object

→ On a mountain summit

→ On a ridge or cliff

→ Near tall trees or other tall objects

→ In gullies, washes, ditches, streams, or any type of water

→ Near large boulders or under rock overhangs (lightning can travel along the rocks to reach the ground)

→ In shallow caves

So what can you do if you get caught in an exposed area with a lightning storm? The first thing to do is to move quickly out of the open, to lower ground if you are high up. Getting below tree line would be best. Make sure you are not the tallest object in the area. The tallest object often receives a direct strike. Do not seek shelter next to the tallest object, either, because the strike can jump from the tallest object to a person standing nearby. Be aware of dangerous ground currents and do not lie down. When lightning strikes a tree, the energy from the lightning strike spreads out along the ground, and it can travel through your body. Stay away from any body of water, which is also a good conductor of electricity.

DIRECT STRIKE   SIDE FLASH   GROUND CURRENT

Avoid any place that might flood in a storm and find a spot among small trees or bushes (remember to stay away from tall trees, large boulders, overhangs, and canyon walls). Once you've found the safest place to stop, assume the lightning position: Put your foam sleeping pad, or any other insulating item you have, on the ground and get on—hopefully, the pad will be enough to break the flow of electricity in case it spreads along the ground. Crouch down on the balls of your feet and keep your feet together to minimize contact with the ground. Tuck your head and cover your ears. Do not hold any metal objects like flashlights or tent stakes.

If you are hiking with a group, spread out at least fifteen feet from one another (about the length of two jump ropes stretched out) so the entire group doesn't get struck by lightning. A lightning strike can damage your brain, burn your skin, and slam your body into the ground, causing even more injury. Although rare, a lightning strike can also stop a person's heart and breathing, and the victim will require CPR. Lightning strike victims have a high survival rate when treated quickly with CPR, so check out some local CPR classes before you head out on the trail.

Did you know that once you get struck by lighting you are more likely to be struck again? A park ranger in Shenandoah National Park was struck seven times!

How Far Away Is That Lightning?

When you see lightning flash outside, count how many seconds go by before you hear the thunder. (You can use your watch if you want.) Sound travels one mile in five seconds, so once you have that number, divide it by five. Let's say you see the lightning and get to ten before you hear the thunder: $10 \div 5 = 2$, so the storm is two miles away. Track the storm with each flash of lightning and rumble of thunder so you can tell whether the storm is moving toward you or away from you. Since electrical storms can move very quickly, the best response is to seek safe shelter as soon as you begin to calculate the time between a lighting bolt and thunder clap. If you are outside and not able to count to ten between a lightning bolt and thunderclap, then you will want to assume the lightning position immediately.

Staying Put

Always wait at least thirty minutes after you hear the last rumble of thunder before you move away from your safe location. Lightning can strike many miles away from where you think the storm is. Sometimes lightning strikes before it looks like the storm is near or when it looks like the storm has passed. Remember, when there's thunder, there's lightning, even if you didn't see the flash.

TRY IT → Lightning Position

STEP 1 Put your pad on the ground.

STEP 2 Squat down on your pad, keeping your weight on the balls of your feet, and your feet together.

STEP 3 Put your hands over your ears and keep your head low.

⬤ **I DID IT!** DATE:

TRACK IT ↘ Lightning Spotting

There are many different types of lightning, and it can be neat to watch it from a safe place. The next time you are in your house or car and there is a storm, see if you can identify what type of lightning you see. Once you determine what lightning type you have seen, draw a sketch to help you remember.

TYPES OF LIGHTNING

CLOUD-TO-GROUND LIGHTNING There are many types of lightning in this category, including forked, bead, ribbon, and staccato.

CLOUD-TO-CLOUD LIGHTNING For example, spider lightning.

INTRA-CLOUD Also called sheet lightning because of the "sheet" of light it produces.

I DID IT! DATE:

CHAPTER 23

Hiking Waterfalls and Slippery Terrain

There is something mesmerizing about a torrent of water cascading over the side of a mountain or down into a ravine. Have you ever hiked just to see a waterfall? Or happened to come across one and have it all to yourself? Here are some ways to make the most out of your next waterfall outing.

LOOK FOR RAINBOWS If the sun is out and you're standing in the right spot, you can see rainbows in the spray and mist.

SEARCH FOR PLANTS Waterfalls create their own distinct environment, or microclimate, where different types of vegetation can grow. Look for moss, flowers, and plants that don't appear anywhere else on your hike.

HUNT FOR SALAMANDERS Waterfalls also create a special place for critters to live. Go to a safe place downstream and gently lift up a few medium-size rocks near the bank of the water. Can you find any salamanders?

QUENCH YOUR THIRST You can filter some water downstream of the waterfall for a refreshing drink. Or you can ham it up in front of the camera by tilting your head back, opening your mouth, and asking a friend to frame the shot so it looks like the waterfall is falling into your mouth.

APPRECIATE THE SOUND There is a reason that so many noise machines have a waterfall setting. Take a minute to close your eyes and just listen to the consistent, soothing rush of water.

Rainbows in Waterfalls

Rainbows are created when white light bounces off the back of water droplets in the air and breaks into all the colors of the spectrum.

That's why they appear when the sun comes out quickly after a storm or when it is partly sunny and raining. Waterfalls can throw a lot of water into the air. So if it is a sunny day, stand with the sun at your back and look in the spray or mist for a band of red, orange, yellow, green, blue, indigo, and violet. You can also look for a pot of gold if you like, but you may have better luck searching for a salamander.

Waterfall Safety Tips

→ Stay on marked trails. Avoid getting too close to the edge of the falls. If you are viewing the waterfall from an observation deck or behind a fence, do not lean over the edge or climb on the railings.

→ Do not climb on rocks around or above the falls. Wet rocks, or rocks with algae, can be very slippery, and a fall could result in a serious injury or even death.

→ If swimming is allowed beneath the falls, check out the surroundings and exercise caution. Strong currents at the base of the falls might pull you underwater. If you jump in, make sure you know beforehand that the water is a safe depth and clear of sharp rocks or branches.

→ Take extra care in cold weather. Remember that rocks, observation decks, and anything that could get wet from the waterfall's spray may be covered in ice.

TRY IT →   Waterfall Hike and Painting

Research your area and find a waterfall hike that interests you. Plan an outing with your friends or family. (It might be a great place to take a picnic lunch.) Sit at the bottom of the falls and enjoy the cool spray of the waterfall. After lunch, use the water near the base of the waterfall to paint on the nearby rocks. You can dip your fingers in the water to draw pictures, write messages, or play tic-tac-toe with a friend.

I DID IT!   DATE:

TRACK IT ↘ Waterfall Sketch

WHAT YOU'LL NEED

➣ A pencil or colored pencils.

STEP 1 Find a nearby hike with a waterfall to explore.

STEP 2 Hike to the waterfall and find a great viewpoint.

STEP 3 Notice the details—the way the water cascades over the rocks and the spray as it hits the water below.

STEP 4 Get sketching on the next page!

 **I DID IT!** DATE:

 TAKE IT TO THE **NEXT LEVEL** ↗

Waterfall Rappelling

Waterfalls are fun to hike to, but sometimes you wish you could get a little bit closer! If you want a close-up view, consider rapelling down a waterfall with a guide. With proper safety equipment and an expert leading the way, you will be able to have an entirely different experience.

I DID IT! DATE:

CHAPTER 24

Tornadoes and Hurricanes

Before heading into the backcountry, always look at a weather forecast. But even if the forecast looks good, nature is unpredictable. The more time you spend outside, the more you will be able to read the weather by the clouds and wind. Perhaps you detect a shift in the wind or maybe the clouds that were puffy and white are now building and getting darker. These are clues that your sunny day just might be turning wet.

Severe Storms in the Backcountry

If you are backpacking for an extended period of time, you might not be aware that bad weather is headed your way. Before you go, find out where outposts such as ranger stations are located along the trail so you can get weather updates. Download a weather app on your phone for the local area so you can get alerts and updates.

Before a major storm hits, there are often clues all around you. The clouds will change and the sky will get darker. Sometimes the air gets cooler or the wind shifts, almost announcing a storm is headed your way. Even the animals give you clues. Look for animals scurrying around trying to take cover. You might notice a sudden eerie silence in the forest. If the animals think it is smart to hunker down, you should, too!

Tornadoes

A tornado is a narrow column of violently rotating wind that extends from the base of a thunderstorm to the ground. It is extremely powerful and can destroy everything in its path. Tornadoes can happen very fast, and they don't always have a visible funnel cloud. Look for these signs:

ROTATING CLOUD BASE

SWIRLING DUST

HEAVY RAIN

→ Rotating cloud base

→ Swirling dust or debris under a cloud base

→ Heavy rain or hail followed by dead calm or an intense shift in direction of the wind

→ Loud, continuous roar like a train

You will not be able to outrun a tornado on foot. If there is a permanent building nearby, seek shelter there. A shelter made of wood is *not* a safe option. And a tent is definitely not a safe place to be in a tornado. Once you are in the safest location possible, assume the safety position. Lie down on your belly or crouch down on your knees and then bend forward with your hands protecting your head and neck.

Being close to the ground makes you a smaller target so there is less of a chance of being struck by lightning or a flying object. The lower you are the better, so find a ditch or low-lying area, and lie flat with your hands covering your head. Try to avoid objects that could become flying debris or a target for lightning, like tall trees.

Once the tornado passes, it does not mean the threat is over. Continue to monitor the situation, including the possibility of more tornadoes or continued severe weather.

Sometimes storms sneak up on you in the woods. You might not even realize a storm is imminent until it's suddenly darker, cooler, or windier. Storms make for poor visibility, and you might only be able to see the trees around you. If you think a storm might be headed your way, don't wait until the last minute to take action. Begin looking around for safe areas while you can see well. Go ahead and put on your rain gear. If you are stuck in a crouched position in the pouring rain for a while, you will get cold. You do not want to be stuck in a storm and dealing with hypothermia, and you can get hypothermia even in temperatures in the 50s if it is wet and windy.

Hurricanes

Unlike tornadoes, hurricanes develop and travel much more slowly. They are huge storms that produce heavy rain, high winds, tornadoes, and flooding. They form in the ocean over warm water and can be catastrophic if they reach land. A hurricane is not usually a surprise because it has probably been tracked for days before it makes landfall. But hurricanes do make unexpected turns, and they create stormy weather far from where the eye (the center of the storm) is.

In fact, a hurricane can be several hundred miles wide! If you are planning a backpacking trip, avoid hurricane weather by looking at the weather forecast before you go. The Atlantic hurricane season is between June 1 and November 30. The eastern Pacific hurricane season is May 15 to November 30. If there is a chance of a hurricane hitting the area, do not go into the backcountry. A hurricane's high winds, flooding, and thunderstorms pose a severe safety hazard.

If you have no access to weather forecasts and you find yourself in a hurricane, use everything you know about storm survival to stay as safe as you can. Of course, if you can get to a secure building, do so immediately. You might even have to change your strategy as the storm evolves. A hurricane often produces tornado outbreaks, so stay alert. Depending on its strength, a hurricane's winds can range from 74 miles per hour (119 kilometers per hour) to more than 157 miles per hour (252 kilometers per hour). Find somewhere to hunker down out of the wind to stay protected from flying debris. A hurricane does not travel at fast speeds, so be prepared to ride it out for a while. It may be several days before you are able to hike out.

TRY IT → Tornado Trial

Go into your backyard or a nearby park and look around. If a tornado were nearby and there were no permanent buildings, where would you go? Go there and practice getting into the tornado position.

I DID IT! DATE:

TAKE IT TO THE NEXT LEVEL ↗

Storm Tracker

If it is hurricane season, do some research and see whether any are forming out in the ocean before going on your next hiking or camping adventure. Track how many days it will take before it makes landfall (and reschedule your trip if you can!). Continue to track the storm as it develops.

➢ How big was the area that was affected?

➢ How was the area where you planned to hike affected?

I DID IT! DATE:

SECTION 4

TRAIL ACTIVITIES

CHAPTER 25

Finding Your Inner Peace

Let's say your friend was supposed to come with you on a three-day backpacking trip, but she came down with a stomach bug and had to bail last minute. Now you are out on the trail with your soft-spoken uncle who likes to walk twenty feet ahead of you. To add to it all, your mom thought this would be a good time to spend three days without your cell phone. This is going to be the most boring three days ever! Or is it? Some people worry that a simple walk in nature might be boring. Yes, there is a chance that you will feel bored on a long hike, but don't worry about it—instead, embrace the boredom. In the woods, you don't have the constant pressure to produce, perform, or react. Most of life is lived in structured environments with structured schedules and lots of expectations. When you step away from that and into nature, it can feel weird and even a little uncomfortable, but you might also realize that what you are feeling isn't actually boredom...but a sense of peace.

Taking a walk in nature might lead to places where you don't have cell phone connection, and that can be one of the best parts of the experience. More and more, studies are showing that excessive screen time might not be the best thing for our brains, our relationships, or our creativity. Hiking where there's no service naturally limits the function of your cell phone. But even if you have a strong signal, put your phone in silent or airplane mode when you are on the trail so that you can feel fully present in your environment.

Earphones on the Trail

Plugging both ears with earphones can be dangerous. Out in nature, your ears are an important safety tool. They can alert you of an animal off trail before you see it. (This is especially important with animals you want to avoid, such as bears, snakes, and skunks!) It is also good to hear other people approaching from behind. If you like to listen to music or audiobooks, use just one earbud and leave the other ear open. You can also listen without earbuds, but the volume should be kept low. Be sure to turn it off when other hikers are around so that they can enjoy the natural sounds of the woods.

Hiking is what you make it. It can be filled with conversation or quiet and restorative. And much like trying out different speeds and hiking styles on the trail, it's a good idea to try different approaches to conversation and entertainment on the trail. At first it might feel like you need to fill the space with talking or music, but the more you are quiet on the trail, the more you may realize that hiking without talking and without entertainment is one of the best ways to come up with great ideas or to clear your mind and give it a rest from your normal, everyday life.

TRY IT → Device-Free Day Hike

WHAT YOU'LL NEED

➣ A day pack with snacks and gear.

STEP 1 Pack up your normal hiking gear but leave all electronics at home or turned off.

STEP 2 Tell someone responsible that you are heading out on a screen-free hike, without the use of a smartphone or other devices. Also tell them where you are hiking and when you will be home.

STEP 3 Complete your hike without the use of any electronic or battery-powered devices, including phones, cameras, and GPS units.

STEP 4 If you are hiking with someone else, be quiet for a large portion of the hike.

STEP 5 Reflect on your experience.

➣ What did it feel like to hike without the use of your devices?

➣ What are some of the noises that you heard?

➣ What did you think about?

➣ Did it feel weird or uncomfortable to be quiet for fifteen minutes?

➣ Did you enjoy it?

➣ Would you want to do it again?

I DID IT! DATE:

TRACK IT ↘ Let Your Mind Wander

Journal about how your mind travels while you hike.

➢ Where does your mind go when you let it wander?

➢ Did you come up with new ideas?

➢ Think about people who are special to you or places you have visited.

➢ Write about what your mind is drawn to.

➢ Include the date and the thing you're most interested in reflecting on.

DATE

I DID IT! DATE:

Hiking Meditation

Even if you turn off all your devices on a hike, it can be difficult to turn off your mind. The trail is a great place to practice a form of meditation where you still or silence your thoughts and let your brain rest from its constant state of thinking and processing.

- ➤ A great way to get started is to match your breathing with your steps.

- ➤ Inhale with each stride of your left foot and exhale when your right foot swings forward.

- ➤ Focusing on the rhythm of your breathing and movement can help make you more mindful of your surroundings.

- ➤ Some people find it easier to meditate when their bodies are moving than when they are at home and sitting still.

I DID IT!   DATE:

CHAPTER 26

Games Using Nature

Soaking in the serenity of nature is one way to enjoy the trail, but the environment around you is full of awesome stuff. Here are a few activities to get to know your environment even better.

What's That Sound?

Trails are very rarely quiet. The sound of wind through the trees, the rushing of a nearby stream, the sound of a runner or mountain biker coming toward you, or the sound of an animal rustling in the bushes—all these noises are unique to a hike. Mastering your knowledge of sound in nature is like a superpower: Try to guess what is making a noise before you turn to look.

→ Tell the type of a tree by the sound of the wind. The noise of wind sounds different in aspen trees than it does blowing through pine needles. Aspen trees sound like they are rustling or quaking; it is a very inconsistent sound. The wind through pines often sounds like a soft and subtle whisper.

→ If you hear water near the trail, listen closely. Try to determine which direction it is flowing and how large the creek, stream, or river might be. Do you think it is flowing fast or slow? How can you tell?

→ Determine what animal is making a noise. Some animals make similar noises as they rustle through the underbrush. A squirrel makes so much noise as it busily scurries from tree to tree that often it can be confused for a larger animal like a deer or bear. Can you tell the difference? Try to imitate the animal call or cry and see whether it talks back to you. Marmots and pikas both communicate with high-pitched chirping, but a pika sounds squeaky and the marmot sounds more like a yell.

→ Identify bird calls, the ultimate auditory identification game. By studying the sounds and habits of local birds at home, you can better recognize them on the trail. You can also pack a pair of binoculars so you can spot the birds after you hear them on your hike. There are several apps and websites that can help you learn and recognize bird calls.

Animal Sightings

Some hikers have a "life list" of animals they're determined to spot in their lifetime. They may want to see rare animals such as a white squirrel or endangered animals such as a black-footed ferret. Instead of a list, choose one special animal that you want to see or find on the trail. It is worth researching that animal's habits and patterns to pick the best possible hikes to see that animal. For example, if you want to see a moose and you find out they are often found near water around dawn or dusk, you can plan an early morning hike to a lake.

Naturalist Apps

There are now apps and online communities that help hikers record their animal sightings in a way that catalogs the information for other hikers and researchers to share. So by playing this game, you are not only going on a backcountry animal safari, but you are also helping compile data that can aid scientists in conservation. Now that's a pretty rad game!

Color Matching Challenge

On your next hike, try to find natural objects that fulfill the basic color categories: red, orange, yellow, green, blue, indigo, and violet.

To step up the challenge, grab a dozen or so paint color sample chips from a hardware store and take them on your next hike. See if you can match these specific hues to the wildflowers, fallen leaves, lichen, rocks, and other colorful features along the trail.

Tree Identification

Touch is also a great way to engage with your environment. Try to identify trees by closing your eyes and touching the bark. Different species of trees have different bark characteristics: A smooth, muscle-like bark is probably going to be a beech tree or hornbeam. A peeling or flaky bark might come from a paper birch. Flat, short evergreen needles that smell like Christmas are from a fir. Deep grooves might mean you are touching a locust. And scaly bark with sap probably means you've found some form of pine tree. Ask a friend to guide you to different tree trunks, as opposed to wandering through the forest with your eyes closed—otherwise you'll most find a poke-me-in-the-eye tree.

KEEPING IT SIMPLE

Simple games like skipping rocks by a lake or drawing in the dirt with a stick can be hours of fun—especially if you have a tic-tac-toe tournament going. One of the best parts of hiking is remembering that you don't need a lot of stuff to be happy—just a little creativity.

TRY IT → Salamander Hunt

WHAT YOU'LL NEED

➢ A camera and a pencil.

STEP 1 Pick a nearby hike with one or several creek crossings to explore.

STEP 2 When you go for the hike, stop at each creek and look for salamanders. Gently lift up rocks that are located half in and half out of the water and look for signs of life.

STEP 3 If you see a salamander, take a picture of it before it squiggles away.

STEP 4 If you don't get a picture, use your memory to draw an image of the salamander below.

STEP 5 When you get home, use your photo or sketch to identify the salamander in a field guide or an online reference. Try to use a resource local to your region, because there are over seven hundred recorded salamander species in the world!

I DID IT! DATE:

TRACK IT ↘

Animal-Spotting Wishlist

Did you know that in certain places lightning bugs synchronize their lights and glow on and off at the same time? Wouldn't that be cool to see? Or what about hiking on the beach and spotting dolphins in the surf? Go ahead and write down a bucket list of outdoor animals that you would love to see in your lifetime.

I DID IT!   DATE:

Guessing Animal Behavior

An excellent way to identify animals in your environment—
even when they are hard to spot—is to learn the different
footprints, or tracks, left by the critters in your region.
Draw the animal tracks you see—hiking after a rainstorm is a
great time to catch lots of footprints. Try to figure out what the
animal was doing—chasing, feeding, switching direction.

I DID IT! DATE:

CHAPTER 27

Games with Friends

Nature can provide entertainment on the trail, but so can your hiking companions. There are several games you can play with a hiking partner that will keep you thinking, guessing, and laughing down the trail.

Sing Aloud

Singing aloud is a common pastime on trails and around campfires. When you tire of singing in unison you can turn it into a game. One person will sing a line from a song, then the next person has to use one word from that line and come up with a line from a different song that uses the same word. The next person now has to pick a word from the song that was just sung and keep the game going. You can play with a time limit of, say, five or ten seconds before a person has to sing a line or lose the game. A less competitive version gives each person as much time as they need to think of a song and keep the game going. This is usually the best option when there are only two players.

Twenty Questions

This popular game allows you to pretend to be anything or anyone. You could be a bluebird or Martha Washington— just make sure you know enough about the thing or person to answer questions.

The other hikers pepper you with twenty questions such as where you live, how big you are, and who you spend time with. If your friends guess who or what you are in less than twenty questions, then they win the game.

Psychiatrist

The game of psychiatrist is all about finding patterns. One person is the designated psychiatrist, who will ask questions of the group after they have had a chance to pick a secret pattern among themselves. The pattern could be something physical such as sniffling before answering a question or looking to the right when it's your turn. Or the pattern could be in the answers to the psychiatrist's questions. For example, one pattern might be to answer the next question with a word that starts with the last letter of the previous answer. So if the last answer was blue, the next answer could be eggs, followed by smart, followed by tarantula, and so on. The psychiatrist asks everyone in the group questions to try to figure out the pattern. The answers may make perfect sense or be completely nonsensical. Either way, there is usually plenty of laughter—and some frustration on the part of the psychiatrist!

Fortunately, Unfortunately

Start the game with a statement such as, "Three friends went for a hike in the woods." Then the next person adds a sentence starting with the word *fortunately*. "Fortunately, it was a beautiful day for a hike, with perfect weather." The next person will add a new line to the story starting with the word *unfortunately*. "Unfortunately, one of the hikers was sick and had to keep running off the trail to relieve himself." The longer you are able to keep the story going, the more fortunate or unfortunate it usually becomes.

Would You Rather

Another game that can keep any group laughing and entertained on the trail is "would you rather." This game allows participants to come up with zany questions that cause participants to think deeply about a world with only two options. One fun spin on this game is to make all the questions trail specific. Here are a few to get you started:

→ Would you rather only hike uphill or downhill for the rest of your life?

→ Would you rather eat only energy bars or only trail mix for a two-week hike?

→ Would you rather hike with someone who talks the entire time or someone who doesn't talk at all? (If the person responds, "Someone who doesn't talk at all," then it might be time to end the game.)

 **TRY IT →** ## Pine Cone Wiffle Ball

Games that you play while hiking usually involve your mind and not many additional objects, but if you are taking a break or are already at camp, you can pull out a deck of cards or play physical games such as pine cone Wiffle ball.

WHAT YOU'LL NEED

➣ A hiking pole or stick and a pine cone.

STEP 1 Establish three bases and a home plate. (Trees or rocks make great bases.)

STEP 2 Designate a pitcher and as many infielders or outfielders as you want.

STEP 3 It's time to play! Roughly following the rules of baseball or Wiffle ball, take turns trying to hit the pine cone as far as possible and see how many bases you can touch before getting tagged out.

 **I DID IT!** DATE:

Hiking and camping are great opportunities to come up with new games or your own versions of tried-and-true classics. Use this space to keep the rules to any great games you come up with.

I DID IT! DATE:

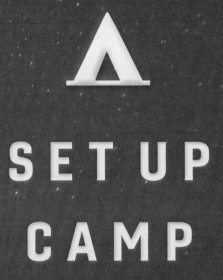

PART III

SET UP CAMP

What would YOU do?

You are on day three of a four-day backpacking trip, and you've stopped at a stream to filter some water. You accidentally drop your filter and the rushing water carries it away. You have two liters of clean water, but that won't be enough to reach the end of the hike. You take out your map—is there a shorter route home? You also have a camp stove and pot that can be used to boil water, but if you boil a lot of water, will you have enough fuel left to cook your dinner, too? What would you do?

SET UP A SHELTER

CHAPTER 28

Scouting the Right Campsite

Finding the best campsite is all about making the best decisions based on the given conditions. If you are walking along a narrow ledge with a steep drop-off when a thunderstorm sneaks up, then you will have limited time and options to make a safe decision. And you might have to backtrack to find safer level ground, even if it takes you farther away from where you want to go. Or if it's a blue sky day, you can scout out different locations to find the most scenic spot for your tent. With enough time you can even lie down on your sleeping pad in a few different spots to test how flat the ground is before picking your ultimate site.

In any circumstance, here are a few things to keep in mind so you can make the best choice possible.

→ Camp at designated or preestablished campsites. Campsites are usually created for a reason—chances are there is a nice level spot for your tent, a nearby water source, a good tree to hang a bear bag from, and a prebuilt ring for campfires.

→ Find flat ground whenever possible, and avoid protruding objects such as rocks, stumps, and roots. Slopes can make sleeping and walking around the campsite difficult. And if it rains, water will run downhill through your campsite. Better yet, look for level ground that is slightly raised, such as a knoll or rounded hill, so you stay high and relatively dry—or at least away from drainage—in heavy rain.

→ Camp 100 yards (91 meters) away from water sources and away from where you cooked, ate, and ultimately stored your food.

→ Don't sleep right beside a privy or outhouse. Hikers using the bathroom in the middle of the night will wake you up. It also might smell horrible if the wind is blowing in the direction of your tent.

→ Choose a campsite that is not under any hazards such as dead trees or branches that may fall in the middle of the night. Even if you are so exhausted that all you want to do is throw up a shelter, climb inside, and fall asleep, take a few minutes to walk around the campsite and identify risks first. That's a whole lot easier than pitching a shelter and then having to take it down and move it.

Makeshift Campsite

You always want to try and stop at designated or preestablished campsites so that you don't disrupt or destroy the plant life along the trail. However, if an unexpected thunderstorm hits or you twist an ankle and can't reach the next official site, then you will need to set up a makeshift campsite.

Here's how to make your own campsite in a pinch:

1. Assess your surroundings and decide the best place to pitch a shelter that will keep you safe and limit damage to the environment.

2. If darkness is falling and you are short on time and daylight, then consider quickly putting up a rain fly or tarp for shelter instead of trying to perfectly set up a tent.

3. Do not try to start a fire unless it is a true emergency situation.

4. If conditions improve, then you can reinforce your shelter or move on to an established campsite.

5. When you leave your makeshift campsite, try to fluff up any vegetation that has been trampled and kick leaves or debris over any sections of dirt that were cleared for your tent. This will discourage future hikers from camping in the same spot.

TRY IT →

Design Your Campsite

Architects and interior designers often sketch out images of buildings and rooms before they turn their visions into reality. Take some time to sketch an overhead view of your perfect campsite. If you take time to draw it, you will be able to recognize sites with similar properties and potential on the trail.

I DID IT! DATE:

Find two different places in your backyard or a nearby park where you might want to set up a campsite. Take your sleeping bag or pad and lie down in each location and answer the following questions:

SITE 1

LOCATION: ....

Are you comfortable when you lie down on your sleeping bag? Why?

....

Would it be a good location if it storms? Why?

....

What is nearby that might be useful for a hiker, such as a tree for a bear bag or a stream?

....

Is the campsite peaceful? (What's nearby that might attract animals or people?)

....

Is the campsite beautiful? How so?

....

LOCATION: ....

Are you comfortable when you lie down on your sleeping bag?
Why?

....

Would it be a good location if it storms? Why?

....

What is nearby that might be useful for a hiker, such as a tree
for a bear bag or a stream?

....

Is the campsite peaceful? (What's nearby that might attract
animals or people?)

....

Is the campsite beautiful? How so?

....

Which location would be the best place to spend the night?

Circle the best option: SITE 1   SITE 2

I DID IT! DATE:

Setting Up in the Dark

Spotting a great campsite in daylight can be tricky—and finding a place to pitch your tent in the dark is even more difficult. If you have a safe place to go outside at night, be it your backyard or a friend's property, then search for a suitable campsite in the dark and practice setting up your tent with a headlamp or flashlight. Practicing your camping skills in the dark will provide you with confidence and a skill set to pick a campsite at night on the trail.

I DID IT! DATE:

CHAPTER 29

Pitching Your Tent

When you set up your tent, your main objectives are to make sure it is pitched properly so it doesn't collapse on you in the middle of the night and to secure it so that it won't shift in winds.

Most tents come with support poles. Some tents have poles that are threaded through sleeves in the tent fabric, while others use poles to make an outside frame that suspends the tent from tiny hooks. Some tents use hiking poles to add tension and shape to the tent. For example, a Rainbow tent uses one long pole threaded through the center of the tent's roof to form an arch. The corners of the tent floor are then spread into a rectangle using either stakes on the outside or hiking poles placed inside along the head and foot of the tent.

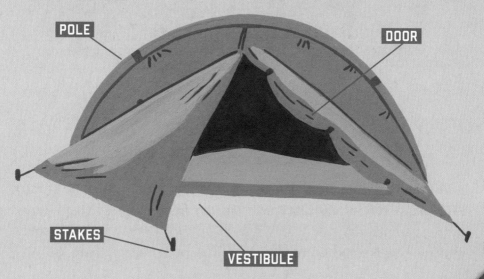

When securing your tent, locate the lightweight tent cords located at the corners and sides of the tent. These lightweight ropes are often referred to as guylines or paracords. With stakes, these cords provide shape and structure to nonfreestanding tents and secure all tents in place. To stake a tent, loop each cord over a pointed metal or plastic stake with a hook on the end to hold the string in place. Most tent cords have tension adjustments that allow you to tighten the line and make the tent fabric more taut once the string is staked down. If there is not a place to tighten the cord, then you can create a tighter hold by looping the cord around the stake several times. If the ground beneath you is hard or frozen then you can use a nearby rock to pound the stakes securely into the ground. But be careful not to bend the stake . . . or smash your finger with the rock!

POLES
UNDER THE RAINFLY

RAIN FLY

VESTIBULE

STAKES

DOOR

INNER TENT

GUYLINES

After the tent is up and secured, make sure the vents and mesh windows are open so that fresh air can flow inside. If there isn't proper ventilation, then you will be way too warm, and if it's cold outside, you'll wake up feeling as if it rained, even if there wasn't a cloud in the sky the entire night. (The warm, moist air from your breathing will raise the temperature inside your tent, and if the moisture can't escape, condensation, or even frost, will form when the warm air hits the cooler tent fabric.)

In a properly designed tent, vents can and should stay open during a rainstorm without allowing any water to enter the tent. But if it is especially windy and the rain is falling at a strong angle, then you might need to close these openings to prevent puddles from forming in your shelter. If you see a rainstorm coming, take a few minutes to make sure that the tent is staked down tight and then go ahead and cinch or close the vents. This should keep you from having to climb out of your tent during a storm to restake one of the tent cords, and it will allow you to make adjustments to the vent openings once you determine the strength and direction of the rain.

If your tent is secure and breathable, then you shouldn't have any trouble sleeping soundly through the night—unless you camp under an oak tree in the fall, in which case falling acorns will keep you awake until sunrise.

TRY IT → Set Up Your Tent

STEP 1 Separate the different parts of the tent. Then make a mental plan on how to best set up the tent. Refer to the instructions as necessary.

STEP 2 Some tents have a groundsheet (or "footprint"); others don't. If there is a thin piece of fabric to use underneath the base of your tent, spread it out where you plan to set up the tent.

STEP 3 Set up your tent poles as directed in the instructions. This may involve inserting the poles into sleeves in the tent fabric to stand it up or setting the poles up as a frame and hooking the tent on to them.

STEP 4 If your tent has an outerwall or rain fly, then set it up over the inner wall structure.

STEP 5 If necessary, stake the tent down by securing the tent cords to the stakes, pulling the corners out diagonally, and then driving the stakes into the ground.

STEP 6 Inspect your tent. Walk around it and make sure the fabric is taut (not hanging loose). Go inside your tent and look around. Is there good airflow? Is any side sagging inward? Without taking it down, make small adjustments such as tightening the tent cords or opening the air vents and mesh windows so it's even more breathable and secure.

I DID IT!   DATE:

Time Your Tent Setup

➤ Set up your tent and time yourself.
How long did it take you?

➤ Setting up a tent well is more important than setting it
up quickly, but there are certain occasions, such as an
approaching storm, when you need to do both.

➤ Try to set up the tent again and see whether you can do it a
little faster. What was your time?

PRO TIP FOR RAINY DAYS If you are setting up a shelter in the
rain, throw your backpack inside the shelter as soon as it is
pitched, before you make any exterior adjustments to the tent
such as tightening the tent cords or driving down the stakes.
Throwing your gear inside the tent as soon as possible helps
keep it as dry as possible—even if *you* are getting soaked!
Practice it at home!

I DID IT! DATE:

CHAPTER 30

Set Up a Tarp

There are several advantages to using a tarp instead of a tent as a camping shelter. Backpacking tarps weigh less than a tent, and they can be set up and taken down very quickly. They are also—for obvious reasons—extremely breathable, and you hardly ever have to worry about condensation. However, a tarp won't protect you from bugs unless you add bug netting, and it won't protect you from wind and precipitation unless you set it up to do so. But there are several different ways to set up a tarp, and you can choose which configuration works best for you, the terrain, and the conditions.

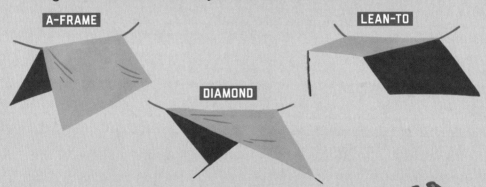

A-FRAME

LEAN-TO

DIAMOND

Looking for Support

Hikers typically rely on trees and trekking poles to lift and support their tarps, but sometimes they are forced to set up quickly and in an exposed environment without trees or poles. Use rocks, fallen branches, man-made structures, or anything else that might help you create a tarp shelter in a pinch.

Tying and Staking Your Tarp

Camping tarps come with multiple built-in tabs, loops, or grommets called tie or guy points. These points allow you to attach trekking poles and cords to the tarp so that you can set it up in different ways, tie it to trees, and stake it to the ground. Some tarps even come with thin paracords preattached to some points (check before leaving home so that you can pack any necessary cord).

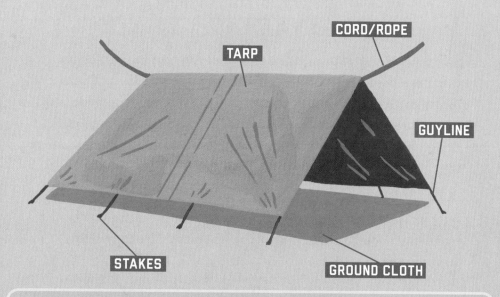

CORD/ROPE

TARP

GUYLINE

STAKES

GROUND CLOTH

Tyvek as a Groundsheet

Most hikers who use a tarp also use a thin groundsheet underneath so that they are not sleeping directly on the ground.

If you are looking for a cheap, durable, lightweight groundsheet to use with your tarp, then go to a hardware store and buy a sheet of Tyvek. Tyvek is a lightweight and flexible material that is used as a moisture barrier in construction. The material can be easily cut to custom measurements, and it can be thrown in a washing machine, which makes it a favorite option for campers.

A-Frame

The simplest tarp configuration is using a rectangular tarp to create an A-frame shelter. The A-frame looks like a traditional tent, with triangle-shaped openings on either end.

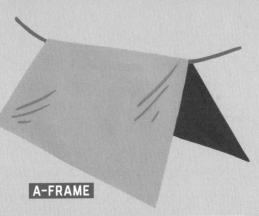

A-FRAME

SETTING UP AN A-FRAME TARP:

STEP 1 Lay out the tarp. Make sure that the four corners of the tarp have cord attached to them. If needed, tie and knot paracord to the corners of the tarp. Locate two paracords in the middle of opposite sides of the tarp. If your tarp has no preattached cords or cords only on the corners, run a loose cord under the middle of the fabric.

STEP 2 Tie these cords to nearby trees, or if there are no nearby trees, then you can use trekking poles to add structure and support to the tarp.

STEP 3 If you use a trekking pole for support, then stake the cord that is running from the top of the trekking pole to the ground. (Using two trekking poles to set up an A-frame tarp is possible with one person, but much easier to do with two people so that one person can hold up the pole while the other stakes the cord to the ground.)

STEP 4 Last, stake out the four corners of the tarp to the ground and voilà! You have an A-frame shelter.

Diamond

On a pleasant night with little chance of rain, you might want to set up your tarp in a diamond.

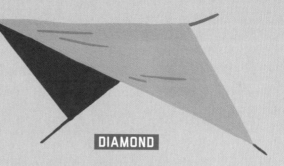

DIAMOND

SETTING UP A DIAMOND TARP:

STEP 1 Lay out the tarp. Make sure that the four corners of the tarp have cord attached to them. If needed, tie and knot paracord to the corners of the tarp.

STEP 2 Tie two opposite corners of a square tarp to nearby trees, as high as possible.

STEP 3 Use paracord to stake down the two loose corners as tight as possible.

Lean-To

LEAN-TO

The lean-to design creates three open sides, but still offers substantial protection from wind and precipitation when pitched properly.

Arrange the tarp configuration so that the wall of the tarp is facing into the wind or rain as opposed to the awning.

SETTING UP A LEAN-TO TARP:

STEP 1 Lay out the tarp. Make sure that the four corners of the tarp have cord attached to them. If needed, tie and knot paracord to the corners of the tarp.

STEP 2 Find the paracords in the middle of the opposite sides of a square or rectangular tarp. If the tarp has no preattached cords or cords only on the corners, you can run a loose cord under the middle of the fabric.

STEP 3 Use the paracord to suspend the middle of the fabric to chest or waist height and tie each end to a tree.

STEP 4 Step to one side of the suspended tarp and stake the corners on that side to the ground.

STEP 5 Step to the opposite side of the suspended tarp. Place your trekking pole under one of the two loose corners and pull the fabric tight. (If your tarp has a grommet or metal hole in the corner, you can place the top of the trekking pole handle on the ground and stick the bottom tip through the grommet.) Then stake the paracord running from that corner to the ground.

STEP 6 Almost there! One more corner to go. Take your second trekking pole and place it underneath the last loose corner of the tarp. Pull the tarp tight and secure the paracord extending from that corner to the ground. Your lean-to tarp is complete with a wall on one side and a roof on the other.

Knots

There are lots of different knots that can be used on a backpacking trip. Here are two knot formations that can be used to tie paracord to the tarp and then secure the paracord to trees or stakes.

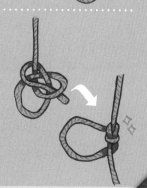

BOWLINE:

A bowline knot helps you form a loop that will not slip. This creates a spot in the cord that can easily be hooked and unhooked around tent stakes.

STEP 1 Make a loop in the cord so that it looks like a lower case b with the loose end of the cord—the "working end"—resting on top where the cords meet, creating a long tail (or superhero cape) for the letter.

STEP 2 Take the working end of the cord behind the neck of the b and then thread it through the backside of the loop.

STEP 3 Now bring the cord to the right of the long neck of the b and wrap it around the back of the neck to reach the left side.

STEP 4 Take the working end and thread it through the front of the loop. This time, keep pulling on the cord while also holding the b at the intersection where its long neck meets its big belly. When you are done pulling, you should be left with a sturdy loop and a knot that can easily be untied.

TWO HALF-HITCH:

A two half-hitch knot can be used to secure cord to the trunk of a tree. It is secure enough to keep your tarp taut all night, but it can be easily loosened and undone in the morning—even with cold fingers!

STEP 1 ▸ Take the cord and wrap it around a tree trunk to make a U shape. If you don't have a tree trunk, you can use any type of round object, such as a broom handle, to practice. It helps if you practice with an actual tarp, or attach the long end of the rope to an anchor, to provide stiffness to the long end of the cord.

STEP 2 ▸ Now take the working end of the cord and place it over the stiff piece of cord to create a loop.

STEP 3 ▸ Pull the working end of the cord underneath the stiff piece of cord, and then bring it back above the intersection of cord that you have created so that it is to the right of the intersection and next to the tree trunk, broomstick, or other object.

STEP 4 ▸ Repeat step 3 below the existing coil to create the second half hitch, then pull tight.

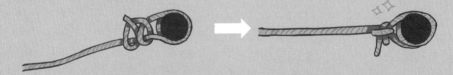

TRY IT → Tarp Variations

WHAT YOU'LL NEED

> An outdoor space with grass or dirt, five feet (one and a half meters) of paracord for each corner of the tarp and a twenty-foot (six meter) stretch of paracord or rope to raise the "roof" of the tarp and tie to nearby trees or hiking poles, four tent stakes,* trekking poles, and a tarp.

* If you don't have tent stakes, use long hardware nails, and if you don't have a tarp, use an old flat bedsheet to practice. If you are not allowed to cut small holes for paracord in the corners of the bedsheet, then tie a simple knot at the end of each corner and tie the paracord behind the knot using a bowline.

STEP 1 Set up each tarp configuration from pages 208–210:

☐ **A-FRAME** ☐ **DIAMOND** ☐ **LEAN-TO**

STEP 2 Which tarp configuration was your favorite? Why did you like it the best?

STEP 3 Clean the tarp by shaking it out in the wind. If it really got muddy or dirty, then you can wash it with a garden hose and mild dish soap. Be sure to let it dry completely before packing it up. (If you used a bedsheet to practice these setups, then throw it in the washing machine to get it clean.)

I DID IT! DATE:

Now that you have practiced setting up three different tarp formations, create a design that is all your own. Given the gear you already have, can you think of another tarp formation that would be useful? Draw it below and then come up with a name. You can create something completely new or combine some of the features from the formations you've learned. For example, you could stake one side of the tarp in an A-frame entrance and prop up the other with a pole like a lean-to. Perhaps attach bug netting to the tarp to prevent pesky insects from coming inside. Or find something to give your tarp shape and structure besides a hiking pole or tree.

TARP NAME:

....

I DID IT!

DATE:

MANAGE CAMPFIRES AND CAMP STOVES

CHAPTER 31

Fire Safety

Fires can keep you warm on a chilly night, help you dry out after a storm, and be used to roast marshmallows. There is something about a campfire that inspires late-night talks, songs, and an occasional ghost story. However, when not tended properly, campfires pose a risk to humans and the surrounding environment. So just remember, starting a fire is a little like having a pet: You shouldn't have one unless you plan to take good care of it.

How to Prep for a Fire

Before you go into the backcountry, contact the local land management agencies where you plan to hike, such as the national forest headquarters or state park office, to check the following:

→ Are there any bans on campfires or camp stoves?

→ Do you need a permit to make a campfire?

→ Are there any particular messages about fire danger on the days you'll be camping?

Use that information to consider whether you can or should make a fire or wait until another trip.

CODE RED

The US Forest Service uses colors to indicate the risk of starting a wildfire. Green fire danger means there's a low risk; blue means moderate; yellow, high; orange, very high. Red fire danger means the risk is extreme and any fire can spread quickly and burn out of control. If an area is in a drought or it is a windy day, you can still sit around and tell stories, but skip the campfire.

Even if the risk is low, take these precautions. You want to enjoy your marshmallows over the fire, but also make sure your fire stays in one place! A metal or rock barrier called a fire ring will help contain the fire and keep the flames from spreading.

→ Always use a fire ring or a protective circle of rocks around a fire to help keep the embers from blowing away.

→ If there's a preexisting fire ring or fire pit, use it. Building a new fire ring is not encouraged by Leave No Trace principles because it leaves a man-made impact where there wasn't one before.

→ If you must make your own fire ring, build it at least fifteen feet (four and a half meters) away from other objects. Before you leave camp, disassemble it and scatter the rocks.

→ Make sure there aren't any leaves, logs, or low branches nearby.

→ Keep your fire to a small, manageable size inside the ring.

→ Always have lots of water nearby and a tool to shovel dirt on the flames if they get out of hand.

→ If you have a pile of wood ready to go in the fire, stack it upwind from the flames.

WIND

How to Finish Your Fire

After you have enjoyed your time around the campfire, do you just head to your cozy sleeping bag and leave the fire to die out? Nope. Never leave your campfire unattended, and never leave it to "burn out" on its own. Winds can easily stir up heat from a dying fire and cause sparks to fly. Remember these rules for extinguishing your campfire:

→ Stop adding wood to the fire well before you plan to go to sleep or leave the area so it begins to die out. Let the wood burn completely to ash if possible.

→ Drown your fire with water! When the water hits the hot coals and ash, it will make a hissing sound and create a lot of steam. Avoid standing where the steam might scald you and keep adding water until you no longer hear this sound.

→ Use a shovel or long stick to stir the ashes, breaking up any large coals and pockets of "live embers" that are orange and glowing. Check if there are any embers hiding underneath any logs or rocks. Add more water and stir again if necessary. Make sure everything is wet.

→ Search the surrounding area for sparks or live embers that may have escaped. If the wind kicks up, they could reignite—and unintentionally start a fire.

→ Don't leave the area or go to sleep until the ashes are cold.

→ When in doubt, add more water!

Pack It Out

Follow the "Pack it in, pack it out" rule. Do *not* take a shortcut and dispose of items in your campfire to avoid having to carry them home. That plan could backfire—literally! Lighters, glass, plastic, gas, and flammable liquid are a few items that could explode, release dangerous toxins, or create excess smoke.

 **Build Your Own Fire Ring—and Take It Apart**

New fire rings should only be built when a fire is allowed and there are no preexisting fire rings in the area. So it's not a skill that campers and backpackers put to use often, but it's still a good one to know how to do!

STEP 1 Head to a nearby trail or forest, or a place in the backyard. (Since this activity doesn't involve starting a fire, you can follow these steps in areas where fires are not allowed.)

STEP 2 Gather twelve to twenty rocks that are bigger than your fist and smaller than your head.

STEP 3 Place the rocks in a circle about a foot in diameter (about the same size as a twelve-inch pizza). Make sure all the rocks are touching and that there are no large gaps in between.

STEP 4 Once you have practiced building your fire ring, practice Leave No Trace and scatter the rocks back in the forest.

 **I DID IT!** DATE:

CHAPTER 32

Building a Fire

Let's face it, sitting around a campfire might be the best part of a camping trip. And building the campfire can be pretty great, too. It's like building with blocks and it is a terrific opportunity to practice being an engineer. But it can also be extremely frustrating when you can't get a campfire going, especially on a cold or damp day. Knowing the best fire-building strategies can help improve your chances of success. Sometimes you can make a couple of small changes and soon have a s'mores-worthy blaze!

The Best Wood for a Fire

As you choose your campsite for the evening, check for a fire ring—if there isn't one, build one (see page 220). You should always have a fire ring, pit, or other protective barrier surrounding your fire. Also, take a look around and see whether there is the right kind of firewood nearby—you should never cut down a tree or break live branches to use in a fire. Live trees do not make good fire starters! They often contain sap or water, and even if you can get them to light, they usually create a lot of smoke.

Also, cutting down trees can be harmful to the health of the forest, and pulling branches and stripping bark can allow insects and disease to infect healthy trees and kill them. Plus, some animals may be using the nearby trees and branches for food and shelter.

Don't cut down a dead tree, either. Dead trees are also important to plants and animals! Dead trees often have holes where animals find shelter, and some animals, like squirrels and raccoons, build nests in them. So if you cut down a dead tree, an animal might lose its home! And even its food! Dead trees may not look like your idea of dinner, but they are vital to insects that feed on cellulose, and those grubs in turn are pretty tasty to all kinds of other animals, like birds and amphibians, even bears. And once a tree falls and the trunk begins to rot, the dead wood becomes food for organisms in the soil that break it down into nutrients that allow new plants and trees to grow.

So where is the best place to find wood for your fire? On the ground! You don't want to disrupt a fallen tree trunk that is decomposing, but you can search for dry twigs, sticks, and branches of varying sizes around your campsite—they all have different purposes:

TINDER Small twigs, dry leaves, needles, wood shavings, and bark will get your fire started. It will usually catch fire easily, but it burns quickly! Collect more tinder than you think you will need.

KINDLING Small sticks (less than one inch [two and a half centimeters] thick) placed next to the tinder will be able to catch fire and burn for a few minutes. Kindling takes longer than tinder to light, but it will also hold the flame longer and provide the heat needed to ignite larger logs and firewood.

FIREWOOD Bigger pieces of wood will keep your fire going until you decide to let it die out. Remember to stack the wood upwind from your campfire.

How to Build a Fire

Place some tinder in the middle of your fire ring. From here, you have several options for how to build your fire, depending on the kind of fire you want:

TEPEE Build a tepee over your tinder with kindling. Make a wide base like a cone, and leave small gaps between each piece and light the tinder. (Airflow is necessary because fire needs oxygen.) After it's lit, add progressively bigger pieces of kindling and then your bigger pieces of firewood. Keep the thickest part of each piece at the bottom. This type of fire creates an intense heat and tends to burn quickly; it might require a lot of maintenance.

LOG CABIN Place two logs parallel to each other around the pile of tinder. Then add two more crosswise on top to make a square. Build up the four sides until it resembles a cabin. Place some kindling on top and in the center before you light the tinder. Once this type of fire gets going, it is usually pretty easy to maintain because it disperses the flames around the square and burns more slowly than more centralized fire formations.

LEAN-TO The lean-to method is a good choice if it is windy. Place a larger piece of firewood next to your tinder so it blocks the wind. Then put the kindling on top of the tinder, so it is protected from the wind.

CRISSCROSS Get a fire going with just your tinder and gently place the kindling around it in a triangle formation. Then stack your firewood on top in a crisscross pattern.

With all campfires, once you light your tinder, blow lightly or fan the base of the fire to increase the amount of oxygen and make the fire burn faster. You may need to add more tinder and kindling to generate enough heat for larger pieces of wood to ignite. These larger pieces are the fuel that will keep the flames going. Remember to keep your fire small and monitor it at all times.

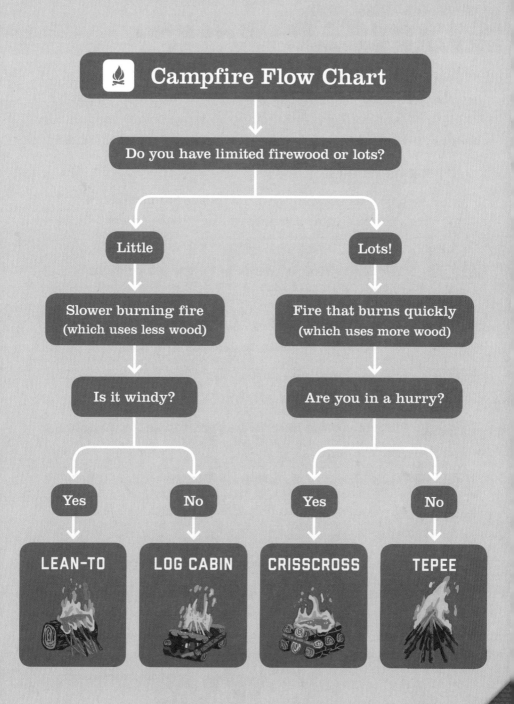

Campfire Flow Chart

Do you have limited firewood or lots?

Little

Lots!

Slower burning fire
(which uses less wood)

Fire that burns quickly
(which uses more wood)

Is it windy?

Are you in a hurry?

Yes

No

Yes

No

LEAN-TO

LOG CABIN

CRISSCROSS

TEPEE

TRY IT → Build a Fire

When you want to do something well, practice! It is much easier to practice under favorable conditions and not when you are cold, tired, and hungry. Practicing the setup before you actually build a fire will help you be more proficient in the backcountry.

WHAT YOU'LL NEED

➤ A place outside where you are allowed to have a fire, matches or a lighter, and several gallons of water.

STEP 1 Build a fire ring if there isn't a preexisting ring, fireplace, or fire pit available.

STEP 2 Collect tinder, kindling, and some bigger pieces of wood.

STEP 3 Practice building each of the four fire types one at a time—but don't light them yet.

STEP 4 Pick one of the four formations to use for an actual fire and rebuild it.

STEP 5 Use a match or lighter to ignite the tinder.

STEP 6 Blow on the fire to help the flames spread and ignite the kindling.

STEP 7 Add larger pieces of wood to keep the fire going.

STEP 8 When you are done enjoying your fire, make sure to extinguish it properly (see page 227–228) by pouring water on top, stirring the ashes, and making sure they are cold before you leave.

I DID IT! DATE:

TRACK IT ↘

Grab a piece of paper and write down a wish or a secret—perhaps it's the one grand adventure that you desperately want to take or it's a friend's secret that has been burning a hole in you. Then use it to start your fire. Watch the pages burn to make your wish come true or release the secret! (Note: Never burn paper that has gloss, wax, or colored ink—it will pollute the area.)

I DID IT! | DATE:

TAKE IT TO THE **NEXT LEVEL** ↗

Put Out a Fire

WHAT YOU'LL NEED

➢ An outdoor fire ring or fireplace, kindling, wood, matches or a lighter, and several gallons of water.

STEP 1 With the help of an adult, start a small fire in the fire ring or outdoor fireplace.

STEP 2 Enjoy the fire—feel its warmth, watch the flames, maybe roast a hot dog or marshmallow. Then it's time to put it out.

STEP 3 Stand upwind of the fire and as far back as you can and still reach it. (Pouring water over fire creates steam, and you want to avoid standing where the steam might scald you.)

STEP 4 Slowly and carefully pour water over the fire until the flames are out. Don't pour too quickly because that can scatter hot embers and splash scalding water onto you. Feel free to take a break and step away if the wind starts blowing smoke and steam your way.

STEP 5 Use a stick to stir the wet coals. You will probably stir up a few embers that are orange and glowing. Pour more water over these live embers and stir.

STEP 6 Repeat steps 4 and 5 until there are no more live embers.

STEP 7 Stay by the fire for another five or ten minutes, checking the area fifty feet around it for any sparks or embers that may have escaped.

STEP 8 Stir the wet coals one more time. If there are still no live embers, you have successfully put the fire out. Congratulations! Now, ask an adult to double-check.

I DID IT! DATE:

SECTION 3

FILTER WATER

CHAPTER 33

Find a Source

One of the best parts of backpacking is collecting and drinking water from natural sources. Bottled water and fluoride-treated city water have caused us to forget that water actually has a unique taste. When it comes from a good natural source, it will taste cold, refreshing, and slightly sweet. Once you learn how to find and treat good water sources on the trail, you might just discover that water from natural sources is far superior to milk, sodas, and lemonade.

But before leaving your campsite, make a plan for when and where you will collect water throughout the day. Running out of water on the trail can be an uncomfortable, even dangerous situation. Always look at your maps and guidebooks and think through the season, recent weather, and potential water sources on the route.

Where to Get Water

All water sources are *not* created equal. If you are anywhere between moderately thirsty to severely dehydrated, then take advantage of the nearest water source. Since almost all water sources on the trail, such as mountain springs, lakes, rivers, ponds, and muddy puddles, will need to be treated or filtered before consumption, even the worst and most unappealling water sources should be safe to drink. In other words, questionable water is better than no water.

If you aren't dehydrated, however, be selective about where you collect water. As a general rule, look for water that is located above roads, livestock, and development. Why? Because no one wants to collect water out of a brown river that is rushing through a valley of cow pastures after a rainstorm! Water rushing through roadside gutters, fertilized farmland, and animal pastures is going to pick up pollution that you won't find near the ridge of an undeveloped mountain. So if you have several water sources to choose from in a relatively short distance, opt for the highest source of water that is located farthest from agricultural fields and development. Bonus points if the water is steadily flowing. Moving water is better than stagnant water that may be covered by a thin layer of pollen or algae.

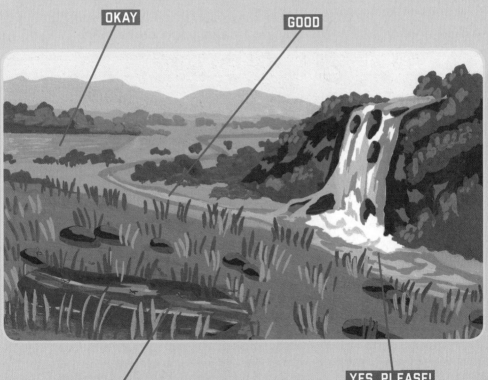

OKAY

GOOD

ONLY IF YOU'RE DESPERATE!

YES, PLEASE!

Consider the Seasons and Weather

Another factor that should be weighed when planning water sources throughout the day is the time of year and recent precipitation. Many of the water sources along hiking trails are seasonal—they run in the spring and dry up by midsummer. If you plan to use small creeks and springs that are listed in a guidebook as seasonal, then carry extra water—especially in dry or hot conditions—just in case a water source is bone dry.

How Much to Carry

You can never carry too much water, right? Wrong! You can absolutely carry too much water. A gallon of water weighs just over eight pounds. Eight pounds! That is the weight of a small watermelon, and no one wants to carry a watermelon in a backpack if it's not necessary. Most hikers will drink around one liter per hour in hot, strenuous, or high-altitude conditions; that's twice as much as easier hikes require.

So, if you are hiking through high mountains in June and finding copious snowmelt, high-elevation mountain lakes, and countless flowing springs, then don't weigh your pack and legs down with unnecessary water weight. You can probably stick to just carrying a liter at a time...maybe a little bit more to be safe. Don't pass numerous high-quality water sources and complain about the weight of too much water in your pack!

TRY IT → Prefilter Out Dirt, Twigs, and Leaves

Having too much sediment in your water can break filters and make it taste unpleasant, so hikers will often prefilter water to remove debris before running it through a purification filter, treating it with chemicals, or boiling it in a pot. All you need to filter dirt, twigs, and small leaf particles out of your water is an extra bandanna or a piece of cloth. Some hikers even use the sleeve of a long-sleeve shirt.

WHAT YOU'LL NEED

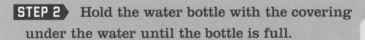

➢ A water bottle, a bandanna or cloth of some kind, and a natural water source such as a spring, creek, river, lake, or pond.

STEP 1 Cover the mouth of your water bottle with the bandanna.

STEP 2 Hold the water bottle with the covering under the water until the bottle is full.

STEP 3 Lift the water bottle out of the water. Remove the bandanna, being careful not to let any dirt fall inside. The water is *not* yet safe to drink, and it may still have a slight color and possibly an odor. But you have successfully removed the grit from the water you plan to use for mac and cheese. And that's a win!

I DID IT! DATE:

TRACK IT ↘

Water Source Bucket List

Collect delicious and pristine water from different types of sources to know your favorite. Here is a checklist of different water sources where you might be able to filter or treat water.

- ☐ trickling stream
- ☐ mountain lake
- ☐ still pond
- ☐ snowmelt
- ☐ spring bubbling up from the ground
- ☐ rushing river
- ☐ downstream of a waterfall

What was the best water?

I DID IT! DATE:

TAKE IT TO THE NEXT LEVEL ↗

River Cleanup

Water is one of our most important resources on—and off—the trail. Every human should have access to clean water, and so should plants and animals. Join a local river cleanup crew in your region to help remove debris from the water. If you can't find a river cleanup, then volunteer to pick up trash somewhere else. After all, most trash that doesn't get picked up eventually ends up in our water.

I DID IT! DATE:

CHAPTER 34

Treat Your Water

The twenty-first century is a great time to be a backpacker, especially when it comes to technological advances in gear—water filters, in particular. There are so many options for treating and sterilizing water in the backcountry that avoiding waterborne illnesses, parasites, and otherwise chunky or brown water is easier than ever. Filtering water removes debris and waterborne illnesses manually. Chemical and UV treatments and boiling will negate harmful agents in the water so that it is safe to drink, but they don't remove anything. Both are good options in the backcountry.

Boil Your Water

Using a fire or your camp stove to boil water for three minutes will kill any living organisms. If you're not planning on sipping something hot or boiling water for cooking, though, it usually isn't worth the time or effort to set up a fire or stove just to boil water for drinking—it'd be better to treat or filter your water. But if you want hot cocoa or tea, boiling can provide safe and piping-hot water.

Chemically Treat Your Water

There are a variety of different chemicals that can be used to treat water, including iodine and chlorine dioxide. The drawback of chemical treatments is that they take twenty to thirty minutes to purify water.

The best and most efficient way to use a chemical treatment is to add it to the water in your bottle and then hike for half an hour before stopping to drink. The shaking required to mix the two will happen with no extra effort as you hike. But before you  drink, let a little of the treated water run through the lid or spout to clean any contaminants that might have been caught in the rim threads when you put the top back on after collecting the water. A downside of using chemicals is that they can leave an unpleasant aftertaste in your water. Iodine in particular can stain your water bottle a brown color. On the upside, chemical treatments are lightweight, affordable, and easy to use.

WHY YOU NEED TWO BOTTLES

Hikers who boil water or use a filter usually carry at least two water bottles or water bladders: one for treated water and the other to collect untreated water. Do not pour water that has been boiled or filtered back into the same bottle that you used to collect the water. Even though the water has been sterilized, it doesn't make the bottle clean. On the other hand, chemical and UV treatments will sanitize the inside of the container carrying the water.

Water Filters

There are lots of kinds of filters—pump filters, gravity filters, squeeze filters, and more. But in each, water is forced to travel through a membrane that removes debris and harmful microscopic organisms. (If you cut into a filter, it might look like porous pumice rock or strands of spaghetti that have been cooked into an inseparable lump.) Filters have become much lighter and more affordable in recent years, making them the top choice for most hikers and backpackers. The drawback is that these filters don't remove viruses, pesticides, or heavy metals. Also, if you use a filter, avoid water with lots of sediment because it can clog or break the filter. To keep the filter working properly, it's a good idea to prefilter water with a bandana or regularly flush the filter with a syringe.

Flush Your Filter

Most filters come with a syringe that can be used to clean the filter and keep it working properly for hundreds and thousands of miles. Here are the steps to flush, or backwash, your filter.

STEP 1 Locate the filter's accompanying syringe.

STEP 2 Put the tip of the syringe into clean, treated water. (Do not use untreated water from a natural source, which could contaminate the syringe and the filter.)

STEP 3 Pull back on the syringe handle to fill the tube with water.

STEP 4 ▶ Place the syringe directly on the side of the filter where clean water comes out, the *back* in *backwash*.

STEP 5 ▶ Use your body-building muscles and push the top of the syringe down with strength to force water through the filter in a strong stream that can dislodge debris and dirt from the inside.

STEP 6 ▶ Repeat steps 2–5 three or four times.

STEP 7 ▶ Now use your filter as intended to purify water for drinking. The water should come out faster and with less effort than before!

UV Treatment

Perhaps the coolest way to treat your water is by zapping it with ultraviolet rays. These water treatment devices look like a lightsaber. When you stick it in your water bottle and push a button, it lights up and sends out ultraviolet rays to sterilize all the bacteria and organisms living in the water. The downside of UV treatment is that it doesn't remove chemicals or odor from the water. And because these devices run on batteries, if you run out of energy, you're stuck without water. So always pack extra batteries or a backup water treatment method.

Do I Have to Treat My Water?

Before modern technology made it so easy to filter or treat water sources in the backcountry, hikers would simply find a good source and drink the water without treating it. Don't take this approach before learning to identify high-quality water sources. One example of a high-quality water source is a high-elevation spring that is far away from buildings, roads, and farm animals. Most people don't want to take the risk, even a small risk, of drinking unfiltered water when it is so easy to treat. But it is fun to remember that until very, very recently, most individuals living and traveling through the wilderness would look for water sources such as mountain springs bubbling up from the earth, and they would drink directly from the spring.

	Boil water	Chemical treatment	UV treatment	Filter
Time needed	Camp stove setup (3 minutes) + bring water to boil (5 minutes) + steady boil (3 minutes) + wait till it cools (7–18 minutes) Total time: 18–29 minutes	Wait 30 minutes	Ready to drink immediately	Ready to drink immediately
Lightweight		✓	✓	✓
Inexpensive (Less than $50)	✓	✓		✓
Removes debris				✓
Taste				Tastes best because it removes debris

TRY IT → Treating Water

STEP 1 Gather water from a natural outdoor source in a water bottle. If you have options, find a water source away from buildings, roads, and farm animals.

STEP 2 Treat the water by using one of these techniques: boiling it at home, using a filter, sterilizing it with ultraviolet rays, or using a dose of chemical purifier.

STEP 3 After you have treated the water, taste it. What do you think?

STEP 4 Find a willing friend or participant to blindfold. Give them a sip of the treated water from outside and a sip of water from the kitchen sink. Can they tell a difference? Which do they prefer?

I DID IT! DATE:

TRACK IT ↘ Journey's End

Much like hikers on a trail, the water you see flowing through your neighborhood and town is on a journey. But where is it going? Find a nearby stream, creek, or river, and do some research using a computer or maps to learn which rivers it connects to and where it eventually empties into the ocean. Then use the space provided to draw a map that traces the journey of that water from your hometown to the ocean.

I DID IT! DATE:

The Gift of Water

Drinking clean water is not just a concern for hikers; it is a
concern for millions of people around the world who don't have
water that is safe to drink in their homes or neighborhoods.
Many water filter companies donate the same filters that hikers
and backpackers use to villages and towns around the world.
When you buy your next water filter, consider buying an extra
filter to donate to an international service group that helps
provide clean water in different countries.

SECTION 4

STORE
FOOD

CHAPTER 35

Food Storage

When you are out hiking for the day and your food is with you, you usually don't have to worry about wildlife approaching you or your food during your lunch break. Critters are often too scared of you to try to steal your peanut butter and jelly sandwich. And if a brave squirrel, marmot, or crow does try to steal a snack, you can usually chase it off by clapping or making loud noises.

But when you backpack and spend the night in the woods, you have to protect your food—and the animals who might want to get it. Rodents will chew right through your bag, backpack, and even your tent in order to get to food. One way to avoid this is to hang a bear bag to protect your food. A bear bag is any sack of food that is hung high off the ground where bears and other critters can't access it. Specialized versions of these bags are designed to keep food scents in and moisture out.

If you are camping, then hanging a bear bag is necessary to keep your food, you, and the wildlife around you safe. Have you heard the expression "A fed bear is a dead bear"? Bears that live in the wild far from people don't eat human food. But when people bring their food into bears' habitats and don't store or dispose of it properly, human food becomes easy for bears to get—and they *will* get it. If you were hungry and could choose between spending your time cooking a delicious meal or having someone hand you one, which would you choose? It's a no-brainer—even for animals. And bears aren't just after your dinner: They will go after toothpaste or lip balm if it has a scent to it, so make sure to store all your scented toiletries with your food.

Once bears associate humans with easy access to food, they might become aggressive. They learn where this food is…at popular campsites, in trash cans, and even in cars! If a bear frequents areas where people are, it often gets the reputation of a "problem" or "nuisance" bear. The unfortunate result is that these bears are often killed, or at least moved from their home.

So to protect the bears, and the food you need for tomorrow, properly hang a bear bag:

STEP 1 Pick the right bag. Your food bag should be durable and waterproof. You might use a nylon stuff sack, dry sack, or other sturdy bag.

STEP 2 Find a good tree! Walk 200 feet (61 meters— about eighty steps) from your campsite. You do not want the smell of food to be in your camp. Look for a tree with a sturdy branch that is clear from other branches (so the rope won't get tangled) and at least seventeen feet off the ground.

STEP 3 Tie a fifty-foot rope to a rock or other weight and throw it over the branch. You could also put a rock in a small bag with a carabiner and attach it to the rope. Make sure the rope is long enough or you could lose it in the tree. Aim for the rope to hang at least five feet away from the trunk of the

200 FEET

tree so an animal can't climb the trunk and reach it. This step might take several tries! Don't get discouraged. If you are with a friend, take turns throwing the rope over the tree branch.

> **SAFETY TIP:** Be careful when you throw the rock over the limb. If the rope is long, it could swing back at you!

STEP 4 After you've thrown the weighted end over the tree branch, untie the weight and attach your food bag. You can either tie the bag with the rope or attach it with a carabiner.

STEP 5 Raise your bag by pulling the rope. It should be at least twelve feet off the ground and five feet below the closest branch. A bear should not be able to reach the bag if it stands underneath. Otherwise, you're just setting up a piñata for the bear.

12 FEET

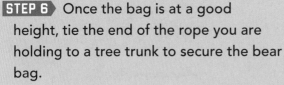

STEP 6 Once the bag is at a good height, tie the end of the rope you are holding to a tree trunk to secure the bear bag.

STEP 7 When you are ready to get your food bag out of the tree, untie the rope from the trunk and slowly lower it to the ground.

Rip-Proof Bags and Dry Sacks

The Ursack is a soft-sided bag, but its weave is tighter and thicker than a regular food bag, and a bear can't rip it open. Many wilderness areas allow Ursacks instead of the heavy, hard-sided bear canisters required in some national parks like Yosemite, where bears are very active. Ursacks are heavier than most food bags, but lighter than a canister. They can be tied to trees, so you don't have to throw a rope over a branch as with a standard bear bag.

Often used by paddlers and rafters, dry sacks keep the water out and hold in food smells better than a traditional nylon food bag or stuff sack. They are a bit heavier than a lightweight nylon bag, but that said, they are still a popular option for food storage and bear hangs on the trail.

TRY IT → Hang a Bear Bag

WHAT YOU'LL NEED

➣ A food bag, snacks, a fifty-foot length of lightweight rope, a rock or other weight, and a tree.

➣ Optional: a carabiner and a small corded bag that will fit the rock (a bag is often easier to tie to the rope).

Follow the steps outlined on pages 245–246, making sure that no people or buildings are near your tree. (You don't want to hit anyone, or any windows, when you toss the rope!)

I DID IT! DATE:

Alternative Food Storage

Campgrounds and wilderness areas have different rules when it comes to food storage—you can't always hang a bear bag. Sometimes the park or management group will require you to utilize another form of food storage. It is also smart to never leave food in your car while you are hiking or camping in the backcountry. You might have an unwanted animal, bear or otherwise, tear into a cooler in your truck bed or break through your car window to grab snacks in the front seat.

Here are some other food storage possibilities. Before you head off on your backpacking trip, contact the agency that manages the area you'll be visiting. Some places require you to have a bear canister or use the provided lockers, cables, or poles if you plan on spending the night.

Bear Canisters

You might hear backpackers complaining about bear canisters because they are heavier, bulkier, and more expensive than a food bag. But they are also more secure. Bear canisters have hard sides and can't be crushed. Although a bear canister is a little trickier to fit into your pack, it is a simple solution for storing your food and scented items. It saves time in the evening since you won't need to hassle with throwing a bear bag. (Plus it makes a great stool and backcountry drum!) Place it on flat, level ground at least a hundred feet from your campsite. Although bears might not be able to get into the canister, they can still swat at it or roll it away, so don't place your bear canister near cliffs or water. And consider painting the lid a bright color so that you can find it if the bear rolls it out of position. You might not be able to find it in the morning! Wedging your canister between rocks or trees can help keep it where you left it.

Bear Boxes

Some campgrounds, trailhead parking lots, and parks provide metal bear boxes for food storage. Simply put your food and scented items inside, close the door, and resecure it. When you leave the area, take everything with you. If there's a bear-proof trash bin nearby, put your garbage there; otherwise pack it out. Bear boxes are not trash cans.

Bear Cables

Popular campsites in woods where bears are common sometimes have permanent cables and pulleys installed among the trees to hang your food bag, or even your whole backpack. These cables have hooks or clasps that attach to your bag, and you pull the cable until your bag is suspended in the air and a securing hook has dropped down. Once you attach the hook to a corresponding eyehook, your bag is secured where animals can't reach it.

Bear Poles

A bear pole is a tall column with metal arms sticking out at the top where you hang your food bag. It might seem simple, but it often takes a few tries to get the hang of using one. You hook your food bag to the end of a separate lifting pole and lift it onto an arm at the top of the bear pole. When you need your food, use the lifting pole to lift your bag off the arm and lower it down.

PART IV

FLORA
AND
FAUNA

What would
YOU do?

You are walking down the trail

enjoying the beautiful day when you turn a corner and see a black bear and her two cubs. They are about fifty feet away, and it doesn't seem like they have seen you. Seeing wildlife is one of the reasons you wanted to come for a hike in the first place. But now that you are actually face-to-face with bears, what do you do next? You think the only way back to the trailhead is to follow the trail beyond the bears, but you're not entirely sure. There is a cliff to the right of the trail and a dense forest to the left making it difficult to walk a safe distance around the bears. What would you do?

ANIMAL SPOTTING

CHAPTER 36

Habitats
(Where to Find Animals)

It is easy to forget that you are walking through animals' homes when you walk through the outdoors. Many trails take you through the habitat, or natural environment, of animals big and small. These places provide the specific needs that each animal requires to survive. For example, you won't find a polar bear in hot and dry southern California (except at the zoo) because it doesn't have the food, temperature, or shelter that polar bears need.

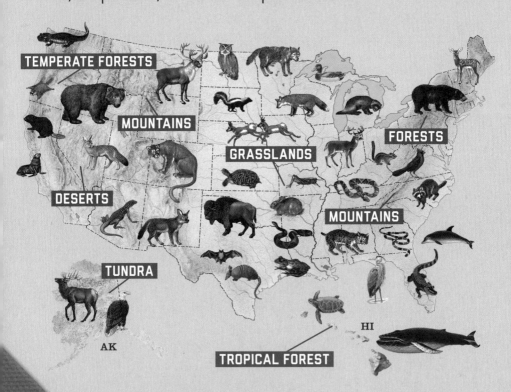

TEMPERATE FORESTS

MOUNTAINS

GRASSLANDS

FORESTS

DESERTS

MOUNTAINS

TUNDRA

AK

HI

TROPICAL FOREST

There are many different habitats in the world, and a trek through some of them will make for pretty amazing hiking trips. You might see plants and animals that live only in a specific environment or notice how the same species can thrive in many different habitats. The gray wolf, for example, once ranged across two-thirds of the United States. It can thrive in the tundra of Alaska, deserts of the Southwest, grasslands of the Great Plains, as well as forests and mountains. Today its range is limited, but if you are hiking in one of the areas where gray wolves have been reintroduced, there's a chance you might see one.

Some park visitor centers have an animal checklist, so see if one is available the next time you go hiking. Here are some animals in a few habitats that you are likely to visit if you are hiking in the United States:

Mountains

The mountains are home to many animals, depending on where you are hiking and at what elevation. Mountainous areas are fun to explore—and there are mountains on all seven continents, so there are plenty to climb! You will often find streams and creeks and beautiful views, as well as forests and open areas of rock and high-elevation meadows.

If you are hiking in the western mountains of the United States such as the Rockies or Cascades, you might get to see bighorn sheep. With their large horns, they are a sight to behold. And maybe you will even have the opportunity to watch a mountain goat kid jump up and down next to its mother on a snow patch.

You might see these animals in the mountains:

MOUNTAIN GOATS

BIGHORN SHEEP

GRIZZLY BEARS

BLACK BEARS

MOUNTAIN LIONS

BOBCATS

WOLVES

DEER

ELK

MOOSE

MARMOTS

PIKAS

RACCOONS

SQUIRRELS

FOXES

SKUNKS

COYOTES

SNAKES

CICADA

ANTS

LADYBUGS

CHICKADEE

BLUEBIRD

Some animals have cool adaptations to help them survive in their habitat. The snowshoe hare has a white coat in the winter to help it blend in with the snow and hide from predators. Then it turns reddish brown in spring and summer to blend in with surrounding vegetation.

Deserts

Deserts are large areas that have sparse vegetation and are very dry. It may not seem like an ideal place to live, but there are many animals that call the desert home. These animals have learned to live without much water. A hike through a desert means you will get to see animals that you won't see anywhere else. And it is hard to beat a desert sunrise or sunset!

Keep your eye out for these animals in the desert:

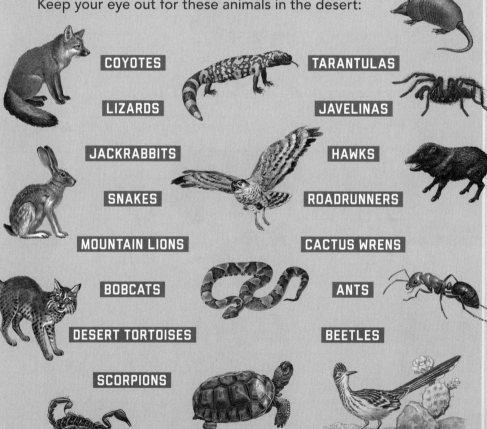

COYOTES

LIZARDS

JACKRABBITS

SNAKES

MOUNTAIN LIONS

BOBCATS

DESERT TORTOISES

SCORPIONS

TARANTULAS

JAVELINAS

HAWKS

ROADRUNNERS

CACTUS WRENS

ANTS

BEETLES

Temperate Forest

A temperate forest remains moderate through all the seasons. It is not extremely cold or hot. You might find pines, oaks, beech, firs, and many more trees. The animals that live in this habitat adapt to cold winters and hot summers. Here are some that you could encounter:

SQUIRRELS

CHIPMUNKS

BOBCATS

RACCOONS

BLACK BEARS

MOOSE

ELK

FOXES

FROGS

SALAMANDERS

DEER

PORCUPINES

OPOSSUMS

OWLS

Grasslands

A grassland (or prairie) falls between a forest and a desert. It doesn't get a lot of rain, but not little enough to be a desert. Guess what the main vegetation is? Grasses! Grasslands are usually open and fairly flat. If you are hiking in the prairies of the Great Plains, you  might get to see pronghorn antelope—North America's fastest land mammal—and American bison—North America's largest land animal. These animals can all be found in grasslands:

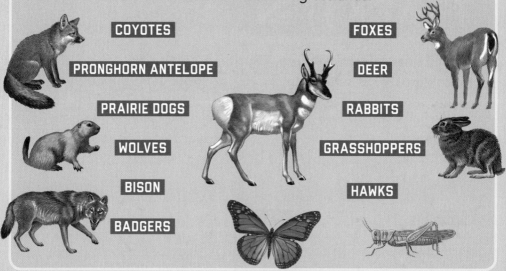

COYOTES

PRONGHORN ANTELOPE

PRAIRIE DOGS

WOLVES

BISON

BADGERS

FOXES

DEER

RABBITS

GRASSHOPPERS

HAWKS

HABITATS WITHIN HABITATS

Just because you live in the desert doesn't mean you won't find green vegetation near a stream with salamanders in it. Grasslands can often contain small clumps of trees scattered across the terrain where a tree-dwelling marsupial such as an opossum might live. These examples are considered habitats within habitats, or microclimates.

TRY IT → Microclimate Safari

Find three distinct local habitats or microclimates, such as a nearby pond, a tree, under a rock, a backyard, a clearing, or the top of a mountain. What animals can you find and identify? Are there any animals that you were surprised to find in these microclimates?

I DID IT! DATE:

TRACK IT ↘

Record any animals you see while on a hike or nature walk. Write down what habitat it was in, and note what it was doing or any interesting features.

I SAW A

WHEN
DATE

WHERE
SPECIFIC LOCATION, HABITAT, APPROXIMATE ELEVATION

WHAT IT WAS DOING

NOTES

I DID IT! DATE:

I SAW A

WHEN
DATE

WHERE
SPECIFIC LOCATION,
HABITAT, APPROXIMATE
ELEVATION

WHAT IT WAS DOING

NOTES

I SAW A

WHEN
DATE

WHERE
SPECIFIC LOCATION,
HABITAT, APPROXIMATE
ELEVATION

WHAT IT WAS DOING

NOTES

I DID IT! DATE:

CHAPTER 37

Tracking Animals and Spotting Scat

Have you ever been hiking—or simply out for a walk—and seen an animal print in the dirt, snow, or sand? Look around you—the animal may still be nearby. What was it? As soon as you step out your door, you are in an animal's territory—not just your own. And you can actually tell a lot about an animal just by its tracks—even narrowing down exactly which animal walked through! Ask these questions whenever you encounter tracks to help you identify your animal:

1. Is the print as big as your hand? Your foot? Is it even bigger than that? Get an idea of the size relative to something familiar.

2. Are there claw marks?

3. Do the back tracks have more toes than the front?

4. Is it a paw or hoof?

5. If it's a paw, how many digits are there?

6. What animals live in this habitat that have the features above?

Hoof Tracks

The most common wild animals with hooves are deer, moose, antelope, mountain goats, boars, bighorn sheep, and elk. And you might come across some bison and cow prints, too! Most animals with hooves usually have a hoof split into two, often referred to as a cloven or split hoof.

BISON

LENGTH: 4.5–6 inches
(12–15 centimeters)

MOOSE

LENGTH: 4–7 inches
(10–18 centimeters)

ELK

LENGTH: 3–4.5 inches
(7–12 centimeters)

COW

LENGTH: 3–5 inches
(7–13 centimeters)

MOUNTAIN GOAT

LENGTH: 3–4 inches
(7–10 centimeters)

BOAR

LENGTH: 2–2.5 inches
(5–6 centimeters)

DEER

LENGTH: 2–3 inches
(5–7 centimeters)

ANTELOPE

LENGTH: 2.5–3.5 inches
(6–9 centimeters)

BIGHORN SHEEP

LENGTH: 3–4 inches
(7–10 centimeters)

Bear Tracks

The first thing you'll notice if you come across a bear track is that it's pretty big! If you find a bear track, put your shoe next to one and compare the size of your foot to the bear's. There is a good chance that the bear's footprint will extend well beyond your sneaker. You can identify a bear track by its five round toes and wide footpad.

To identify a black bear's tracks versus a grizzly's tracks, look at the shape of the print and the toes and claw marks. A grizzly track is more square and a black bear print is more round. If you drew a straight line under the big toe along the top of the footpad of a grizzly track, it would pass the little toe along the bottom. On a black bear track, it would cross the little toe along the top. A grizzly's toes are also closer together than a black bear's, and because a grizzly's claws are longer, the claw marks are farther away from the toe pads.

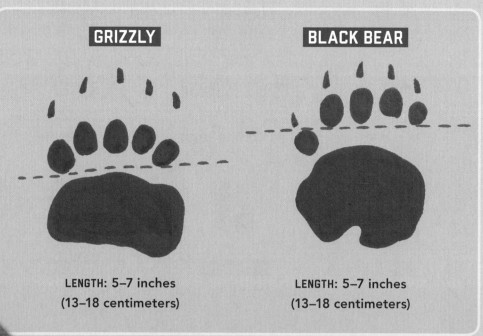

GRIZZLY

LENGTH: 5–7 inches
(13–18 centimeters)

BLACK BEAR

LENGTH: 5–7 inches
(13–18 centimeters)

Canine Tracks

You will probably recognize canine tracks because dog prints are common on and off the trail. But dogs aren't the only canines. Coyotes, foxes, and wolves all have prints similar to a dog. Canine prints have four toes, and the two in the middle are usually side by side. The footpad has a single lobe in the front, and the back is usually indented. Claw marks are almost always visible.

DOG
LENGTH: 1–3.5 inches
(3–9 centimeters)

COYOTE
LENGTH: 2–3 inches
(5–7 centimeters)

WOLF
LENGTH: 3.5–5 inches
(9–13 centimeters)

FOX
LENGTH: 2–2.5 inches
(5–6 centimeters)

Bird Tracks

Yes, most birds fly. But they have to land somewhere, and some spend a lot of time walking on the ground. And if you see two identical prints side by side, the bird is probably hopping.

TURKEY
LENGTH: 3.5–5 inches
(9–13 centimeters)

GROUSE
LENGTH: 1.5–2 inches
(4–5 centimeters)

CROW
LENGTH: 2–3 inches
(5–7 centimeters)

Other Common Tracks

There are many other tracks you might see in the woods. Some animals, such as rabbits and raccoons, have different-size front and back feet. That is another clue that might help you identify an animal. Take a look at these distinct front and back tracks for your next hike!

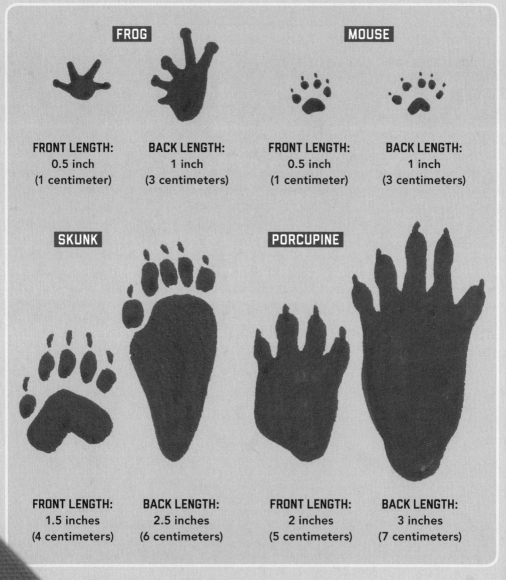

FROG

FRONT LENGTH:
0.5 inch
(1 centimeter)

BACK LENGTH:
1 inch
(3 centimeters)

MOUSE

FRONT LENGTH:
0.5 inch
(1 centimeter)

BACK LENGTH:
1 inch
(3 centimeters)

SKUNK

FRONT LENGTH:
1.5 inches
(4 centimeters)

BACK LENGTH:
2.5 inches
(6 centimeters)

PORCUPINE

FRONT LENGTH:
2 inches
(5 centimeters)

BACK LENGTH:
3 inches
(7 centimeters)

OPOSSUM

FRONT LENGTH:
1 inch
(3 centimeters)

BACK LENGTH:
2 inches
(5 centimeters)

SQUIRREL

FRONT LENGTH:
1.5 inches
(4 centimeters)

BACK LENGTH:
2 inches
(5 centimeters)

RACCOON

FRONT LENGTH:
2.5 inches
(6 centimeters)

BACK LENGTH:
4 inches
(10 centimeters)

RABBIT

FRONT LENGTH:
1 inch
(3 centimeters)

BACK LENGTH:
4 inches
(10 centimeters)

Scat

What is scat? Animal poop! Where is it? Everywhere! Which makes it easy to walk down the trail and play a little game of "what kind of scat is that?" It is amazing how much you can learn from a pile of scat. You can tell whether the animal is healthy and what the animal was eating. It might even help you figure out where to camp—or more likely, not camp. For example, if you come across several large piles of fresh bear scat, you should probably, well...scat! If the animals enjoy living in that area, or mark it as their territory, it is probably best to keep moving on a bit before setting up for the night.

If you come upon the scat of a predator, it will likely contain hair and bones from its prey. If it's not a predator, the scat will most likely have seeds or berries. When it's berry season, bear scat will have a lot of berries and vegetation. Sometimes it even looks like a big pile of cow manure. If there are flies around it or it is warm (don't touch it—just put your hand nearby to feel if heat is radiating off it), the bear is quite possibly close by.

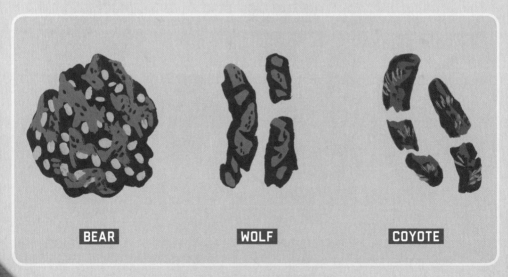

BEAR   WOLF   COYOTE

Some other common poop you'll see is deer, rodent, and cat scat. And you can distinguish these by their shape and size. Animals in the deer family often deposit scat in clusters of pellets. Rodents also make pellet-shaped scat although it is much smaller.

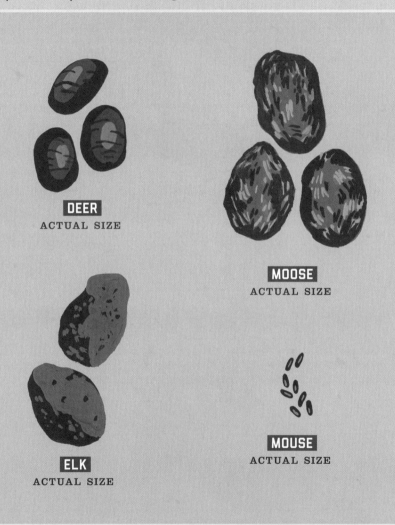

DEER
ACTUAL SIZE

MOOSE
ACTUAL SIZE

ELK
ACTUAL SIZE

MOUSE
ACTUAL SIZE

Most cats have tubular scat that is separated into segments and will likely contain fur and bones.

BOBCAT
ACTUAL SIZE

MOUNTAIN LION
ACTUAL SIZE

ANIMAL SPOTTING

WHAT YOU'LL NEED

≫ Index cards, and a pen, pencil, or marker.

STEP 1 Draw an animal track on one side of the index card.

STEP 2 Write the name of the animal it belongs to (or draw a picture of the animal) on another index card.

STEP 3 Repeat steps 1 and 2 until you have two cards for each animal in this section. Add other animals if you want!

STEP 4 Mix your cards up and lay them out face down. If you are with a partner, take turns flipping over two cards at a time until you find a match.

◯ **I DID IT!** DATE:

TRACK IT ↘ Track Spotting!

Go on a hike to look for tracks or scat, and draw your findings
in the space below. Try to sketch the track or scat to scale by
using the ruler on the back cover, and pay attention to
details like seeds or nail length, which will help you
identify the animal. Use the examples in the previous
pages or do some online research to identify your find.

I SAW EVIDENCE OF A

WHEN
DATE

WHERE
SPECIFIC LOCATION,
HABITAT, APPROXIMATE
ELEVATION

NOTES

I SAW EVIDENCE OF A

WHEN
DATE

WHERE
SPECIFIC LOCATION,
HABITAT, APPROXIMATE
ELEVATION

NOTES

I SAW EVIDENCE OF A

WHEN
DATE

WHERE
SPECIFIC LOCATION, HABITAT, APPROXIMATE ELEVATION

NOTES

I SAW EVIDENCE OF A

WHEN
DATE

WHERE
SPECIFIC LOCATION, HABITAT, APPROXIMATE ELEVATION

NOTES

I SAW EVIDENCE OF A

WHEN
DATE

WHERE
SPECIFIC LOCATION, HABITAT, APPROXIMATE ELEVATION

NOTES

I SAW EVIDENCE OF A

WHEN
DATE

WHERE
SPECIFIC LOCATION,
HABITAT, APPROXIMATE
ELEVATION

NOTES

I SAW EVIDENCE OF A

WHEN
DATE

WHERE
SPECIFIC LOCATION,
HABITAT, APPROXIMATE
ELEVATION

NOTES

I DID IT! DATE:

TAKE IT TO THE **NEXT LEVEL** ↗

Make a Casting of an Animal Track

WHAT YOU'LL NEED

- Water, a plastic bowl, a plastic spoon, plaster of paris, and a small shovel.

STEP 1 Find nearby animal tracks (sandy or moist soil works best).

STEP 2 Dig a trench around the track to keep the plaster from spreading.

STEP 3 Prepare the plaster. In the plastic bowl, mix one part water to two parts plaster. It will begin to harden soon, so move quickly to step 4.

STEP 4 Pour the plaster over the animal track.

STEP 5 Let it sit for thirty to forty-five minutes.

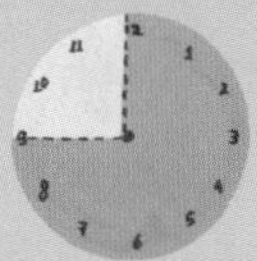

STEP 6 Dig under your mold and remove it from the ground.

STEP 7 Once the track is dry, wipe the dirt off your animal track cast. Voilà! You have a permanent animal track to bring home. Use the mold to identify your animal track if you haven't already!

I DID IT! DATE:

CHAPTER 38

Identifying Calls and Sounds

You probably already know that bees buzz, bears growl, and sheep baa. And, depending on where you live, you might even be able to hear some of these animals in your own backyard. But entering the backcountry will introduce you to a whole new set of sounds. Animals make sounds and calls to communicate with other animals, attract mates, and warn others to stay away. Growl, rattle, hiss, honk, squeal . . . knowing the noises in nature will give you a heads-up about who may be just around the bend.

Noises to Know

You are snoozing soundly in your sleeping bag when all of a sudden your eyes pop open. What was that sound? Chances are, you have been woken up by a coyote—or maybe even a pack. They can be found in most of the United States. Coyotes can make several sounds, but it is quite something to listen to a pack of coyotes howl. In fact, a coyote is sometimes called a song dog. They are also known for their high-pitched barks or yips. Coyotes don't usually approach humans, but if you feel threatened, make a lot of noise and never run from them.

One of the most terrifying sounds you might hear is the rattle of a rattlesnake. You probably won't see the snake because it is so well camouflaged, so when you hear the sound, the hair on the back of your neck stands up! You are grateful for the warning—it is a sound you will never forget. When a rattlesnake holds its tail up and shakes the rattle, it is warning predators to stay away. The snake can also make a hissing sound to scare off unwanted company. Move away from the snake so it doesn't feel threatened.

The growl sound that everyone expects is actually not the sound that bears usually make. Sometimes they grunt or click their tongues. These are not usually aggressive sounds. If the bear is nervous, or feels threatened, it will let out air in a huff or make deep sounds. Sometimes it clacks its teeth. Bears can also moan and make crying sounds—and we don't really know why. Maybe they are just having a hard day? A scared baby bear can even sound like a human baby crying!

Mountain lions are stealthy and quiet. But when they do make noises, it's unmistakably scary! A mountain lion can pierce the air with a high-pitched scream. A mountain lion might also growl and hiss. One of the surprising sounds they make are chirping sounds that sound like baby birds. That is one way they communicate to other mountain lions. And, of course, they purr. They are (very big) cats after all.

Another sound that can make you stop in your tracks is the call of the elk. Known as a "bugle," you will probably consider it more of a scream. It is a very high-pitched sound that seems otherworldly as it echoes through the forest. Bull elks will bugle to find a mate and make it known that they are in the area. They might also be warning other bulls to stay away. The elk makes a lot of other sounds like grunts and even a chuckle. An elk will bark to warn the others of danger. But when an elk bugles, you will take notice!

Screeeeech! If you've ever been woken up by that sound, a screech owl was visiting your campsite. But it usually only makes a screeching noise when it is scared. These owls trill to keep in touch and make barking calls when they are annoyed or worried. Screeches usually occur when they are defending their homes or babies. Barred owls can be identified by their questioning hoot that sounds like "Who cooks for you?" And the barn owl uses many high-pitched screams to talk to other owls.

SCREECH OWL   **BARRED OWL**   **BARN OWL**

There are also many peaceful animal sounds in the forest. There is something almost magical about walking along as songbirds sing their tunes. It is almost like they are welcoming you into their home. And what about the deep call of the bullfrog before you hear the splash as it jumps into the lake? Or the plop of a fish as it jumps out of the water. And, of course, there are crickets singing their lullaby as you fall asleep in your tent. That being said, whether or not the chattering of a squirrel is peaceful might be up for debate!

You don't have to be out in the woods or on a mountaintop to observe animal sounds. You probably hear animals from your driveway, back porch, or maybe even inside your house. Take a few moments to be still and listen. You just might be surprised at what you hear!

Pick two times a day to stop and listen for animals. It might be morning and night. Or maybe you want to see whether any animals are active in the middle of the day. Record your findings below.

TIME 1

What does it sound like?

What is the animal?

TIME 2

What does it sound like?

What is the animal?

I DID IT!   DATE:

TRACK IT → Animal Sounds

Track any animals you hear on a hike or nature walk. Include date, time, where and what type of habitat, what it sounded like, and any other interesting finds like what the animal was doing or how other animals reacted.

I HEARD A

WHEN
DATE AND
TIME OF DAY

WHERE
LOCATION
AND HABITAT

WHAT IT SOUNDED LIKE

NOTES

I HEARD A

WHEN
DATE AND
TIME OF DAY

WHERE
LOCATION
AND HABITAT

WHAT IT SOUNDED LIKE

NOTES

I HEARD A

WHEN
DATE AND
TIME OF DAY

WHERE
LOCATION
AND HABITAT

WHAT IT SOUNDED LIKE

NOTES

I HEARD A

WHEN
DATE AND
TIME OF DAY

WHERE
LOCATION
AND HABITAT

WHAT IT SOUNDED LIKE

NOTES

I HEARD A

WHEN
DATE AND
TIME OF DAY

WHERE
LOCATION
AND HABITAT

WHAT IT SOUNDED LIKE

NOTES

I DID IT!   DATE:

SECTION 2

WILDLIFE

CHAPTER 39

Large Mammals

One of the most exciting parts of hiking can be animal sightings. Seeing an animal in a zoo is neat, but there is something special about getting to see an animal in its natural habitat. It is only when you walk through nature that you get to see the owl swoop down to catch its prey, the mountain goat jump up and down on the snowfield, or the moose run out of the woods across the trail in front of you.

Before you head off into the wild, find out which animals will be your neighbors on your backpacking trip. Although it is fun to see animals, remember that they are wild creatures and that you are visiting their home. Respect all wildlife by keeping an appropriate

SAFE WILDLIFE DISTANCES

75 FEET (23 METERS)

DEER
AND MOST
OTHER
WILDLIFE

(ABOUT 2
BUS-LENGTHS)

BEARS   **300 FEET (91 METERS)**   (ABOUT 8
BUS-LENGTHS)

distance between you and the animal. If you are in a designated park, rules are usually posted. Often a sign will indicate how far away you should be to view different wildlife safely. Do some research and learn how to behave in the different situations in which you may encounter animals on the trail—if they have babies nearby, if they are eating, if you surprise them, if they attack, etc.

Bears

Seeing a bear in the wild is almost magical. Bears often run away when they hear noise, but seeing them climb a tree or walk through the woods is a rare glimpse into the wild. Bears are one of the largest animals you could encounter, and your adrenaline will probably kick in. As incredible as they are, you should never purposefully get within a hundred yards of a bear. Keep the animal's path clear, so it does not view you as a threat and it can move away.

Bears have an incredible sense of smell and can smell food from miles away! They are most active early in the morning and in the evening. Keep in mind that bears might be hanging around berry bushes as well.

Black Bears

You can find black bears in at least forty of our fifty states. They live in forests and mountains; they walk through small towns and suburban backyards and they have even been found in the swamps of Florida! Black bears don't have to be black, either. They range in color—black, brown, blond, or cinnamon. You can identify a black bear by the straight profile of its face, prominent tall ears, and high rump.

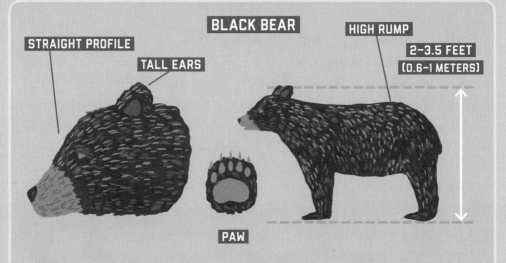

BLACK BEAR

STRAIGHT PROFILE

TALL EARS

HIGH RUMP

2–3.5 FEET
(0.6–1 METERS)

PAW

On all fours, black bears are usually 2–3.5 feet tall (0.6–1 meter). Black bears can climb trees and run up to 30 miles (48 kilometers) per hour. So if they challenge you to a race, then they will probably win.

If you come across a black bear *do not*:

→ **run away (it will probably chase you)**

→ **climb a tree (bears can climb trees)**

→ **give it food (a fed bear is a dead bear)**

→ **play dead**

If the bear hasn't seen you, slowly move away and give it space to go about its business. If it is nearby and sees you, talk calmly so it knows you are a human. Slowly wave your arms above your head and make yourself look big. Often this is enough to send the bear on its way. If you are in a group, stay together. If the bear

is standing still, slowly move away sideways; if you walk backward, you might trip! But if the bear starts coming toward you, stop and hold your ground. Never put the bear in a position where it feels trapped. And never put yourself between a mama bear and her cubs. If she thinks you are a danger to her little ones, she might attack.

In the unlikely scenario that a black bear attacks, *do not* play dead. Fight back with your trekking poles, a rock, or whatever you have. Aim your kicks and punches toward the bear's face.

Grizzly Bears

A grizzly is a majestic animal that can only be found in a few places in the United States—such as Alaska, Montana, and Wyoming. Like black bears, they can be different colors. A grizzly is larger than a black bear, at 3–5 five feet (1–1.5 meters) tall on all fours, with a distinctive shoulder hump. Grizzlies have short, round ears, and dish-shaped faces, and their rump is lower than their shoulders. Their claws are longer than a black bear's. They are around four inches long!

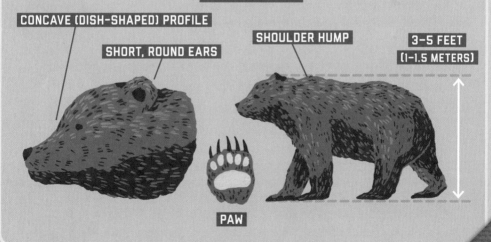

GRIZZLY BEAR

CONCAVE (DISH-SHAPED) PROFILE

SHORT, ROUND EARS

SHOULDER HUMP

3–5 FEET (1–1.5 METERS)

PAW

When hiking in grizzly territory, carry bear spray. It should be somewhere that you can grab quickly—not buried in your pack. And know how to use the spray before you actually need to use it. Also, make noise and hike in a group. When you talk or call out, you are alerting a bear to your presence and avoiding the chance of a surprise encounter (not just for you, but the bear, too). Some people even like to clap their hands! Pay very close attention near streams, rivers, and waterfalls or when there's high wind as bears might not be able to hear you coming. When going over a hill or rise, or turning a blind corner, yell out to announce your presence. If you come across an animal carcass, leave the area immediately. Bears will often feed on dead animals, and even if you don't see any in the area, they may be nearby or returning.

If you are attacked by a grizzly bear, use your bear spray. If it continues to charge, play dead (this is the opposite of the advice for a black bear). Fighting back usually makes the attack worse. Keep your backpack on to protect your back. Lie facedown on your stomach with your hands behind your neck. Keep your legs apart to make it more difficult for the bear to flip you over. You want to protect your stomach and vital organs. Try to stay still until the bear leaves. Grizzly bears often attack to eliminate a threat. If you fight back during an attack, it usually makes the attack more intense. If the attack continues, there may be a point when you need to fight back. Be very aggressive and direct your attack at the bear's face.

Moose

If you have ever seen a moose, you might have first thought, "Wow, that's a huge deer!" Then maybe you noticed its broad snout, the flap of skin under its throat, and its long, spindly legs and realized it was a moose! Moose do belong to the deer family and, at 5–6.5 feet (1.5–2 meters) tall at the shoulder, are the largest of the deer species. They have long faces, and males have huge antlers. Moose are comfortable on land and in water, and you might see them munching on their favorite foods around the edges of lakes, rivers, and marshes. Because they cannot sweat, they can't tolerate high temperatures for long, so you'll only find them in the northern regions of the United States.

Keep a safe distance from moose, at least 25 yards (22 meters). Never put yourself between a mother and her baby. Moose can be aggressive if you are too close, if they feel threatened, or if they are protecting their calves. If a moose charges you, it wants you out of its territory. So get out of its territory! (You probably won't outrun a moose—they are very fast!) Quickly put a tree or some object between you and the moose. A moose can run up to 35 miles (56 kilometers) per hour—even faster than a bear—and it can knock you down with its hooves. If it does knock you down, curl up in a ball and protect your head.

Mountain Lion

A mountain lion is also called a panther, puma, or cougar. Mountain lions can live in the forest, desert, and mountains. They are found primarily in the western part of the United States, and there's a small group in Florida. Mountain lions are very fast and have powerful hind legs that allow them to jump up to 15 feet (5 meters) high (the height of a one-story house) and 40 feet (13 meters) long (the length of a school bus). Mountain lions quietly stalk their prey before ambushing it. Their powerful jaws usually go after the neck.

Mountain lions tend to be elusive and avoid humans, but here's what to remember if you do encounter one:

→ Do *not* run away. Mountain lions can reach speeds of 40–50 miles (64–80 kilometers) per hour, and their instinct is to chase things that run.

→ Back away slowly, and stand up tall.

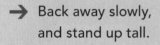

→ Do not crouch down or bend over. The mountain lion might mistake you for prey.

If the mountain lion comes toward you, take these measures:

→ Put your arms in the air and make yourself look big. Open up your jacket if you are wearing one. Slowly wave your arms.

→ Talk in a loud voice.

→ Throw rocks or branches in its direction, but do not crouch down or turn your back.

→ Fight back! If you are attacked by a mountain lion, protect your head and neck and fight using anything you have and with all your might.

When you have a surprise encounter with an animal, you might not have a lot of time to think about what you should do. Your response will mostly be instinct, so practicing how you will react ahead of time will help you in the moment. Cut out the flash cards on the following pages and write the correct response to encountering each animal.

➤ Have a partner stand across the yard from you.

➤ Walk toward them, and when you get about fifteen feet (five meters) away, your partner will hold up one of the animal pictures.

➤ As soon as you see what it is, practice reacting to the situation.

(This is also a great way to memorize the differences between a black bear and grizzly—mix them up and you'll do the exact opposite of what's necessary.)

I DID IT! DATE:

BLACK BEAR

WHAT TO DO: ....
....
....
....
....
....
....

GRIZZLY BEAR

WHAT TO DO: ....
....
....
....
....
....
....

MOUNTAIN LION

WHAT TO DO: ....
....
....
....
....
....
....

MOOSE

WHAT TO DO: ....
....
....
....
....
....

CHAPTER 40

Identifying Insects

If you love science and creepy-crawly insects, you're in luck! With the exception of a freezing-cold winter hike, you are almost guaranteed to see an insect or two (or many more) while out on your hike. In fact, they might "bug" you a lot! It's estimated there are ten *quintillion* individual insects living on our planet on any given day.

Insects make up over half the world's known species. There are over a million different types of insects, and they come in all different shapes, sizes, and colors. But all insects have three body parts—the head, thorax, and abdomen—six legs, and two antennae. They can eat plants or animals. Sometimes they even eat blood (nobody likes getting bitten by mosquitoes)!

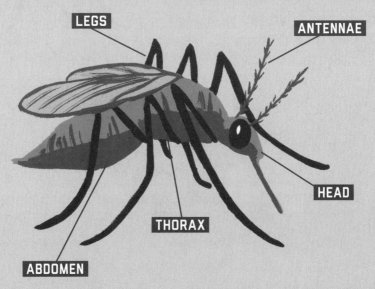

Some people view insects as pests because they have had to fight swarms of gnats or run from a wasp. But insects do a lot of good. Some insects pollinate flowers, and others eat harmful insects. Silkworms, the larvae of a moth, make . . . you guessed it . . . silk! And in some parts of the world, insects are considered to be a delicious food. Sometimes they are even dipped in chocolate!

Not that you should eat that ant that crawls on your candy bar the next time you are sitting on the ground enjoying your snack. But maybe pay more attention to these tiny, but way cool, creatures. Here are a few common insects you will most likely encounter on your next adventure outside:

ANTS Ants live in organized colonies where each ant has a purpose. They communicate, share labor, and work together. Ants can carry things that are many times their own body weight. And fire ants even have an amazing survival strategy. When faced with high water, ants link together using their legs and mouths to form a raft. The queen ant is protected in the middle as the "raft" floats. Now that is taking care of your family!

BUTTERFLIES AND MOTHS Butterflies are beautiful creatures and a delight to see as you are hiking along. They are found all over the world except for Antarctica. The patterns on butterfly and moth wings are made of tiny scales. Some butterflies migrate with the seasons. Monarch butterflies embark on a journey that is thousands of miles!

A moth looks similar to a butterfly, but its colors are usually not as bright. It also has different antennae and a thicker, hairier body. Butterflies are active during the day while most moths fly at night.

BEES AND WASPS Many people are afraid of encountering bees and wasps while on the trail. A sting from either can leave a painful reminder. A bee will die after it stings, but a wasp can sting more than once. Wasps, which include yellow jackets and hornets, are slender and smooth with a narrow "waist," while bees are rounder and have hair.

BEETLES All kinds of beetles can be found in most habitats (again, not Antarctica), which makes these creatures an easy find on lots of hikes. The dung beetle is amazingly strong. It finds poop and eats it and even lives in it sometimes! Ladybugs are a type of beetle.

They come in different colors, but you are probably familiar with the ones that have a tiny red-and-black body. Many people consider ladybugs to be good luck. Maybe that is because they protect crops by eating plant-eating insects. Did you know that a firefly is a beetle? Maybe you have spent summer evenings watching the night sky come aglow. Also known as a lightning bug, a firefly flashes light in patterns to attract a mate. Some beetles can destroy entire forests. Mountain pine and spruce beetles burrow under the bark of a healthy tree, destroying its defenses, and lay eggs, which produce larvae that burrow even deeper, disrupting the tree's flow of food from its needles to its roots. Other bark beetles can introduce diseases that kill trees.

SYNCHRONOUS FIREFLIES

Some fireflies are capable of simultaneous bioluminescence (say that three times fast), which means they flash at the same time. These fireflies are found in a handful of locations around the globe, and a few are here in the United States. You can observe their spectacular light show for a couple of weeks each year on the Tennessee side of Great Smoky Mountains National Park, Congaree National Park in South Carolina, and the Allegheny National Forest in Pennsylvania.

CICADAS When a large group of these insects are gathered together, it can be overwhelmingly loud! Cicadas can live up to seventeen years in the ground feeding on plant roots before emerging as adults with transparent wings to breed and lay eggs for a few weeks before dying. All that noise in the summer is from males "singing" to attract a mate!

PRAYING MANTIS The fascinating praying mantis is a carnivore. It is named for the way it holds its long front legs in a position resembling prayer. Mantises are usually green or brown and are well camouflaged in the plants as they wait for prey to come along. Then they quickly grab the grasshopper or fly or other insect with their front legs and pin it down to eat.

TRY IT → Bug Spotting

See bugs everywhere!

STEP 1 Go outside and sit quietly for five minutes.

STEP 2 Look around you.

STEP 3 Check off any of these that you observe:

- [ ] bug flying
- [ ] bug making noise
- [ ] bug eating
- [ ] bug with wings
- [ ] bug crawling
- [ ] bug building or carrying something

STEP 4 Get up and walk around. Do you see any other bugs? How many can you find in only another five minutes?

I DID IT! DATE:

TRACK IT ↘ Bug Sketching

Go outside and look for insects and draw your findings on the following pages. Insects are pretty easy to find, so pick any destination, even your backyard. Try to sketch the insects to scale by using the ruler on the back cover. If you have colored pencils, they will come in handy—insects can be colorful if you look closely enough. Note any of their behaviors or actions, and perhaps how many legs they have if you can count them in action. When you get home, see whether you can identify any of the unknown insects.

I SAW A

WHEN
DATE
AND TIME
OF DAY

WHERE
LOCATION,
HABITAT,
APPROXIMATE
ELEVATION

NOTES

I SAW A

WHEN
DATE
AND TIME
OF DAY

WHERE
LOCATION,
HABITAT,
APPROXIMATE
ELEVATION

NOTES

I SAW A

WHEN
DATE
AND TIME
OF DAY

WHERE
LOCATION,
HABITAT,
APPROXIMATE
ELEVATION

NOTES

I SAW A

WHEN
DATE
AND TIME
OF DAY

WHERE
LOCATION,
HABITAT,
APPROXIMATE
ELEVATION

NOTES

I DID IT! DATE:

CHAPTER 41

Reptile and Amphibian Spotting

Some reptiles are easy to spot while others might prefer to remain unseen, which makes these mysterious animals an exciting find. Reptiles are cold-blooded vertebrates with dry scales covering all or part of their bodies—the scales vary from microscopic, as on tiny geckos, to the large bony plates of crocodiles. Because these animals don't maintain a constant body temperature, they use the environment to get warmer or cooler. They will move into the sun or onto a warm rock to heat up or go into the shade to cool down. Here are a few common reptiles that you could spot sunbathing or skittering away on your next outdoor adventure:

LIZARDS Lizards can be found in a variety of habitats—deserts, rocky areas, forests, etc. They are fun to watch as they dart all over the place. Sometimes when you are hiking, they run out right in front of you or even under your feet! Lizards are usually active during the day because they use the sun's heat to warm them up.

TURTLES You have probably seen a turtle at some point in your life. They often wander into backyards, or into the road, or sit on logs by the side of a lake. Perhaps when a turtle saw you, it pulled its head inside its shell until you left. Or maybe it plopped off a log and into the water. One of the oldest reptile groups, turtles come in all different sizes and live in a variety of habitats. The box turtle often lives on land, but in mostly moist areas. Sea turtles make their way through ocean currents. Tortoises, which are a type of turtle, live exclusively on land and have round feet that are good for walking or digging burrows when it gets too hot. Snapping turtles have powerful jaws and a powerful bite.

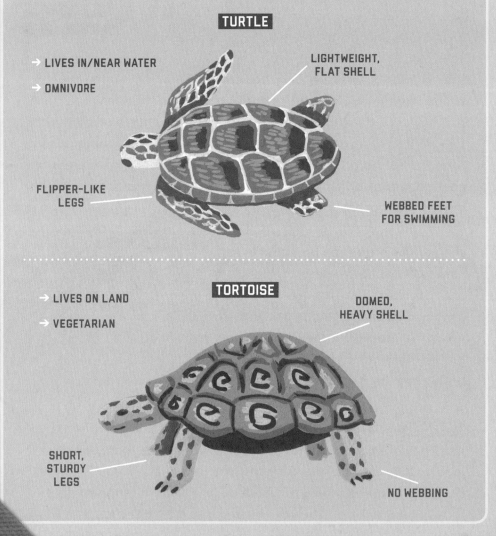

TURTLE

→ LIVES IN/NEAR WATER

→ OMNIVORE

LIGHTWEIGHT, FLAT SHELL

FLIPPER-LIKE LEGS

WEBBED FEET FOR SWIMMING

TORTOISE

→ LIVES ON LAND

→ VEGETARIAN

DOMED, HEAVY SHELL

SHORT, STURDY LEGS

NO WEBBING

Tortoise Fight!

Do you know how a desert tortoise makes it known who is boss? The animals fight until one flips the other on its back. The one who doesn't get flipped over is the winner.

SNAKES Snakes usually prefer to go about unnoticed. But you might find them sunning themselves on rocks to warm up or hiding underneath a ledge in the shade to cool down. Never put your hands or feet somewhere you can't see! Even if snakes are in plain sight, they are masters at camouflage. Give a snake plenty of distance. A snake can strike from a distance of up to half the length of its body!

There are many nonvenomous snakes that you might see on the trail. If you are in the United States, the venomous snakes you could encounter are rattlesnakes, copperheads, water moccasins (cottonmouths), and coral snakes.

SNAKE STEP

Before you step over a fallen log or rock on the trail, put your trekking pole on the other side and look before you step. Snakes often nestle up against these objects and might be surprised into biting you if you step on or near it.

Snakes flick their forked tongue to smell the air, which alerts them to danger or to food. Some snakes don't see well, but they are able to sense heat and feel vibrations. Some snakes can eat animals up to three times their size because they can open their jaws very wide.

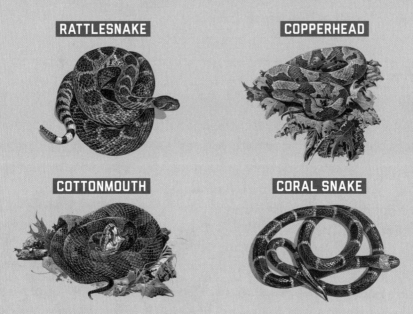

RATTLESNAKE

COPPERHEAD

COTTONMOUTH

CORAL SNAKE

ALLIGATORS If your trekking takes you to the southeastern United States, you might see alligators in marshes, swamps, lakes, rivers, ponds, bayous, etc. Alligators are strong swimmers with powerful tails. Alligators sunbathe to warm up and go into the water to cool off. *Do not* get close to an alligator. They are large, carnivorous animals. Avoid swimming in known alligator habitats, and don't splash; an alligator may think you are injured prey. Be alert when you are filtering water near a source, especially at dawn or dusk. Crocodiles can also be found in south Florida. They are usually found in brackish and saltwater habitats.

AMPHIBIANS Amphibians, like frogs and salamanders, are also cold-blooded animals. They need water or a wet environment to live because they absorb water through their thin skin. *Amphibian* means "two lives." These animals start out in water with tails and gills. They develop lungs and legs in order to adapt to their adult life on land.

At some point you will probably see a frog or toad on your hike. They might hop out of your way, or maybe they will stay very still hoping you won't be able to see them. A salamander is another cool animal you might see. Salamanders look kind of like lizards, but have the moist skin of a frog. There are many kinds of salamanders, ranging in different sizes, colors, number of legs, and the way they breathe. The salamander's habitat varies based on what kind it is. Some spend a fair amount of time on land, but they need to have water nearby. Many salamanders live in humid forests. Their bright colors are a warning to predators. A type of salamander called a newt can even regrow lost limbs.

HELLBENDER

The largest salamander in the United States is the hellbender. They are anywhere from twelve to twenty-nine inches long. They have flat bodies and heads, paddle-shaped tails, and slimy skin. They are nocturnal, so they are often found under rocks during the day, and they come out to hunt at night. Hellbenders like shallow, clear, rocky streams. They tend to be found in areas with fast-flowing water. The hellbender even has a funny nickname: snot otter!

(ABOUT 4 PENCIL-LENGTHS)

TRACK IT ↘

Spotting Reptiles and Amphibians

> ### WHAT YOU'LL NEED
> ➤ A pen or pencil.

Do you see any reptiles or amphibians?
Some will be easy to spot and some will be hiding in plain sight. And others might be hiding under rocks or in the water.

STEP 1 Go outside to a nearby park or take this book on your next hike.

STEP 2 Keep your eyes peeled for any reptiles or amphibians.

STEP 3 Record your findings in the space below.

I SAW A

☐ REPTILE   ☐ AMPHIBIAN

WHAT WAS IT DOING?

WAS IT EASY TO SPOT?

SKETCH A PICTURE OF THE ANIMAL AND ITS SURROUNDINGS.

I SAW A

☐ REPTILE   ☐ AMPHIBIAN

WHAT WAS IT DOING?

WAS IT EASY TO SPOT?

SKETCH A PICTURE OF THE ANIMAL AND ITS SURROUNDINGS.

I SAW A

☐ REPTILE   ☐ AMPHIBIAN

WHAT WAS IT DOING?

WAS IT EASY TO SPOT?

SKETCH A PICTURE OF THE ANIMAL AND ITS SURROUNDINGS.

I DID IT! DATE:

CHAPTER 42

Bird-Watching

Birds are amazing creatures. They are found all over the world, come in every size and color, and have an incredible range of behavior. A bee hummingbird is only two inches long, and an ostrich can be nine feet tall! Some birds have a permanent, year-round home while others migrate to take advantage of better weather and more food and nesting options. When birds do migrate, some travel short distances or maybe even just change elevations. Other birds travel thousands of miles!

Living Fossils

Based on fossils that have been found, birds and dinosaurs share many features. Some scientists even believe that birds are a type of dinosaur. Think about that the next time you go bird-watching!

Identifying Birds

Identifying birds can be tough because there are over two thousand species of birds in North America alone. Color is often the first thing people look at when trying to figure out what kind of bird they are watching. But you'll probably need to look beyond the color and look at the shape and size of the bird to identify what family it is in. To narrow down your choices even further, take note of these characteristics:

COLOR/COLOR PATTERN
SILHOUETTE/SHAPE
SIZE
BEAK SHAPE
BIRD BEHAVIOR
BIRDCALL
HABITAT

Take a few moments to watch what a bird is doing. A bird's behavior will give you a good clue about its identity. Some birds swim, and some can dive under the water. You might watch birds hop up and down and others run. Some birds are unable to fly. Penguins, for example, don't fly, but boy, are they cute waddlers and expert swimmers. And if you see a bird hammering its beak against a tree, there is a good chance that it is a woodpecker looking for food.

Some birds live only in certain regions or in particular habitats, so take note of your surroundings. Knowing the types of birds that live in an area before you head out will help you narrow down your choices when trying to identify one on your hike. There are birds that live near the ocean that you will not find inland. Some birds thrive in meadows and fields, but are not found in forests or mountaintops. What about identifying marks? Does the bird have spots? Stripes? Special patterns and colors? Like bird-watchers, birds also use these markings to determine whether a bird is a member of their species.

What else is unique to different types of birds? Their songs! If your best friend calls you on the phone, you probably recognize the voice as soon as you hear "hello." After a while, you might be able to recognize a bird by its song even before you see it. The following birds have calls that sound like actual words, which makes them easy to remember and identify in the woods:

BARRED OWL — *Who cooks for you?*

BOBWHITE — *bob-white*

GREAT HORNED OWL — *Who's awake? Me too.*

NORTHERN CARDINAL — *birdie, birdie, birdie*

OVENBIRD — *teacher-teacher-teacher*

Another sound to listen for is the sound of loud thumping or something that sounds like the rotating of helicopter blades. If you are hiking along and hear that sound in the woods, it is likely the ruffed grouse. The drumming is the grouse on a log or rock, its wings beating rapidly. The sound starts slowly and picks up speed. It is a strange sound when you are in the middle of nowhere!

The Cheeseburger Bird

There is a bird that taunts hungry hikers with its song of *cheese-bur-ger.* Of course that isn't what the bird is actually saying, but it is what many hikers hear when they are out in the woods and wishing they had some town food! And of course, the bird's real name is not actually cheeseburger bird. If you hear that three syllable song in the west, it is probably the mountain chickadee. In the east it is likely the Carolina wren.

MOUNTAIN CHICKADEE

CAROLINA WREN

TRY IT → Bird Spotting

Birds are everywhere. Get outside and see for yourself!

STEP 1 Go outside and sit quietly for five minutes.

STEP 2 Look all around you—including at the sky and tree branches above.

STEP 3 Check off any of these that you observe:

- ☐ birds flying
- ☐ birds singing
- ☐ birds eating
- ☐ birds preening
- ☐ birds building or carrying something
- ☐ birds hopping

I DID IT! DATE:

TRACK IT ↘ Bird Journal

Go look for birds on a nearby trail and draw your findings in the space provided. Try to sketch the birds to scale by using the ruler on the back cover. If you have colored pencils, they will come in handy—the patterns on a bird's body and head are an important clue to identification. Note the shape of the beak and any behaviors or actions. When you get home, see whether you can identify any of the unknown birds.

I SAW A

WHEN
DATE
AND TIME
OF DAY

WHERE
SPECIFIC LOCATION,
HABITAT, APPROXIMATE
ELEVATION

NOTES

I SAW A

WHEN

DATE
AND TIME
OF DAY

WHERE

SPECIFIC LOCATION,
HABITAT, APPROXIMATE
ELEVATION

NOTES

I SAW A

WHEN

DATE
AND TIME
OF DAY

WHERE

SPECIFIC LOCATION,
HABITAT, APPROXIMATE
ELEVATION

NOTES

I DID IT! DATE:

Bird Mnemonic Devices

There are some great animal sound libraries on the internet where you can listen to the sounds different animals make. List the birds you most want to identify below. Listen to their birdcalls and, next to each bird's name, write some phrases to describe what you hear—like *cheeseburger*! These phrases will help you remember them the next time you hit the trail.

BIRD

MNEMONIC

I DID IT! | DATE:

PLANT IDENTIFICATION

CHAPTER 43

Trees and Shrubs

Learning to identify different trees and shrubs can be a great skill for a hiker and camper. If you run out of toilet paper on your next backpacking trip, then you could look for a striped maple tree since its leaves can double as toilet paper in a pinch. Knowing how to identify mountain laurel, rhododendron, and azalea shrubs can help you avoid using their wood to build a fire since they can emit an unhealthy smoke. And did you know that you can make a healthy and delicious tea from the twigs of a birch tree? The same is true for the fresh green needles on a hemlock tree.

The first step to becoming an expert tree spotter is to become familiar with the trees where you live and what they look like in each season. If you are traveling through the Sonoran Desert, then you might be better off learning the different types of cactus and sagebrush than common trees of North America, since broadleaf trees are few and far between there. If you are hiking in Great Smoky Mountains National Park in Tennessee and North Carolina, you have the chance to spot 134 different species of trees—and if you want bonus points, hike in the winter and identify most of those trees without any leaves on the branches!

Regardless of whether you live in the Rocky Mountains, where forests are often dominated by one species such as pine or aspen, or hike in the Deep South, where you'll see the greatest diversity of trees in the country, knowing trees gives you access to a whole other side of nature! If you can spot a fruit tree, you can pick the fruit when it is in season. And if you can tell that an ash tree is dying, you'll know not to pitch your tent underneath it.

Sometimes you will find the same kind of tree thriving in different environments, but trees are usually adapted to a specific habitat. As you are hiking and traveling in different areas, keep an eye out for trees in these habitats:

GRASSLANDS OR PRAIRIES Cottonwoods, willows, oaks, and ash trees can be found where water runs through these generally dry landscapes dominated by grasses.

OAK

COTTONWOOD

DESERTS Joshua trees, junipers, bristlecone and pinyon pines, ocotillos, and mesquite trees all have adaptations that allow them to survive in the extreme conditions of the desert.

JOSHUA TREE

JUNIPER

OCOTILLO

MOUNTAINS The trees in mountainous areas vary depending on elevation. In the east, where the Appalachian Mountains are older and lower, you will see fir, red spruce, beech, yellow birch, maple, pine, sourwood, oak, and hemlock. In the west, where the Rockies, Sierras, and other ranges are much higher, you will find pine, spruce, and fir trees, as well as cottonwoods and aspens.

SPRUCE **BEECH** **ASPEN**

Broadleaf versus Conifer

Beyond habitat, a major clue to the identification of a tree is its leaves. Trees fall into two main categories: broadleaf and conifer. Broadleaf trees have...you guessed it, broad leaves! These trees tend to be deciduous, meaning they replace their leaves every year. A few broadleaf trees, such as magnolias and live oaks, keep their leaves all year long. They naturally grow in more mild climates.

BROADLEAF
(Maple)

CONIFER
(Red spruce)

Conifers have leaves that look like needles or scales. They don't usually drop their leaves each year, so they are commonly called evergreens. Producing seeds in cones, conifers include such trees as pine, spruce, fir, and cedar. The giant sequoias of California, the largest trees in the world, are also conifers.

Although there are a few exceptions—such as the bald cypress, which is a conifer that loses its leaves each year, thus the name *bald*—for the most part if you see a living tree without leaves in the winter, you can be pretty sure that it belongs to the broadleaf family.

Once you decide whether a tree is a broadleaf or conifer, here are some further clues to help identify the specific type.

A Closer Look at Leaves

You can often figure out what kind of conifer you're looking at by examining its leaves up close. Pine needles are flexible and grow in bundles (known as fascicles). A white pine has five-needle fascicles,

CONIFER

Cedar scales   White pine needles

and you can remember that because the word *white* has five letters in it. Spruces have stiff, pointy needles that grow individually on a branch. With four sides, a spruce needle is easy to roll with your fingers. Fir needles also grow singly but are soft and flat and do not roll easily. Cedars have tiny overlapping scales that resemble the skin of a snake.

The leaves of broadleaf trees are less straightforward than conifers, having a variety of shapes and configurations. (If you are identifying trees in the winter, look around the base of the tree to examine leaves that have fallen.) Understanding these distinguishing leaf characteristics can help you identify broadleaf trees:

1. SIMPLE VERSUS COMPOUND

Does a leaf stem have one blade or several blades growing from it? One blade per stem is a simple leaf, like a maple or oak. Compound means a leaf is divided into several blades, or leaflets. Hickory, walnut, buckeye, and locust trees have compound leaves.

SIMPLE

COMPOUND

2. OPPOSITE VERSUS ALTERNATE

How do the leaves or leaflets grow from the twig or stem? If they grow directly across from each other in pairs, like a mirror image, then they are opposite. If they do not line up but are staggered, then they are alternate.

OPPOSITE

ALTERNATE

3. LOBED VERSUS UNLOBED

How is the leaf shaped? Does it have major indentations like a glove or a star? Then it's lobed. Compare leaves from an oak and a birch, for example. The oak leaf has

LOBED

UNLOBED

several major indentations that create lobes extending out like fingers of a glove, whereas a birch leaf, although serrated, has no major indentations and looks like a pointed egg or a even a fist. The tulip poplar has lobed leaves that look a bit like stars, while a willow has unlobed leaves that look like a straight lance.

4. PINNATE VERSUS PALMATE

How are the lobes or leaflets arranged? Like a feather, on each side of a single stem? If so, they are pinnate. Locust leaves are pinnately compound, and oak leaves are pinnately lobed. Or are they like fingers around the palm of a hand? If so, they are palmate. Buckeyes have palmately compound leaves, and maple leaves are palmately lobed.

PINNATE

PALMATE

Of course, there are more characteristics to take note of such as whether leaves have straight or serrated edges or are smooth or glossy or fuzzy, but understanding those four distinguishing characteristics will help you narrow down your choices as you search for your leaf or look up descriptions in tree identification guides.

Texture

The bark of a tree can also help give you hints about what type of tree it is. Some trees, like locusts, have deep grooves in the bark. Other trees, like shagbark hickory or sycamore, seem to be shedding their bark. Aspens are easy to recognize because of their smooth white bark.

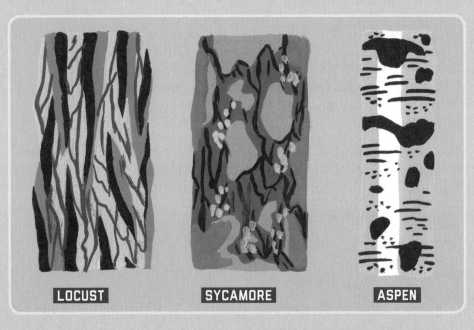

LOCUST   SYCAMORE   ASPEN

One of the best ways to get to know a tree is to touch the bark while you examine the tree. Touching a tree doubles the sensory signals that record the tree's different properties in your brain—your body will remember the tree by interacting with it.

Shape

If you can't get close enough to examine leaves or bark, recognizing tree silhouettes and their general size will help you identify trees from a distance. In general conifers will look more like a tall and narrow triangle, similar to the shape of a Christmas tree. The tops of broadleaf trees tend to be fuller and bushier. They typically resemble a circle, square, or rectangle rather than a triangle.

Pairing silhouette and size with habitat and location, you could narrow your choices down considerably. For example, tulip poplar trees have very straight trunks that point up to the sky and grow to be incredibly tall—usually seventy to a hundred feet, sometimes even taller. So if you see a tall, straight, broadleaf tree in a forest somewhere in the eastern United States, then there is a good chance that it is a poplar.

BALSAM FIR

BEECH TREE

There are lots and lots of different trees, so the best way to start learning their names is to go outside and practice identifying the trees around you right now. That way, when you go hiking, you will probably be able to identify a few trees that you have at home— or their close relatives—and you can expand your knowledge from there.

TRY IT → Pressing Leaves

Become familiar with leaves by preserving them at home.

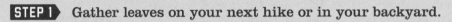

> **WHAT YOU'LL NEED**
>
> ➢ Different leaves, a few sheets of paper, heavy books, wax paper, an iron, and two clean rags.

STEP 1 Gather leaves on your next hike or in your backyard.

STEP 2 Place a piece of paper on a flat surface and arrange individual leaves on top in a single layer. Cover the leaves with a second sheet of paper.

STEP 3 Place a heavy book or two on top of your paper-and-leaf sandwich.

STEP 4 This is the hardest part... Wait twenty-four hours or more for the leaves to flatten.

STEP 5 Once the leaves are flat, place them between two sheets of wax paper.

STEP 6 Preheat the iron to medium. Cover your ironing surface with a rag, and place the leaves and wax paper on top. Cover the layers with the other rag to protect the wax.

STEP 7 With the help of an adult, gently run the iron over the cloth to melt the wax and affix the paper to the leaves.

STEP 8 Trim the excess wax paper from the leaves.

STEP 9 Look on the internet or in a field guide to identify which type of tree each leaf is from.

I DID IT! DATE:

TRACK IT ↘ Tree Spotting!

Two hundred years ago, naturalist William Bartram would head off into the woods to study nature and record the many different plant species he found. He would draw pictures and write descriptions in a notebook. If he found a tree or plant that he couldn't identify, then he would compare his notes and drawings with other field guides and ask for help from people who knew more about the plants than he did.

It's your turn to be a naturalist like William Bartram. Record the trees you see on your hikes. You can even go back and see how the tree changes throughout the seasons!

I SAW A

WHEN
DATE

WHERE
BE SPECIFIC IF YOU
WANT TO REVISIT IN
A DIFFERENT SEASON

BROADLEAF OR CONIFER?

SHAPE

DESCRIBE ITS LEAVES OR NEEDLES

DESCRIBE THE BARK

I SAW A

WHEN
DATE

WHERE
BE SPECIFIC IF YOU
WANT TO REVISIT IN
A DIFFERENT SEASON

BROADLEAF OR CONIFER?

SHAPE

DESCRIBE ITS LEAVES OR NEEDLES

DESCRIBE THE BARK

I SAW A

WHEN
DATE

WHERE
BE SPECIFIC IF YOU
WANT TO REVISIT IN
A DIFFERENT SEASON

BROADLEAF OR CONIFER?

SHAPE

DESCRIBE ITS LEAVES OR NEEDLES

DESCRIBE THE BARK

I SAW A

WHEN
DATE

WHERE
BE SPECIFIC IF YOU
WANT TO REVISIT IN
A DIFFERENT SEASON

BROADLEAF OR CONIFER?

SHAPE

DESCRIBE ITS LEAVES OR NEEDLES

DESCRIBE THE BARK

I DID IT! DATE:

TAKE IT TO THE NEXT LEVEL ↗

Winter Tree Spotting!

Up the tree-spotting ante by testing your knowledge
on a winter hike. Without leaves, you'll only have the shape
of the tree, the bark, and the pattern of the limbs, branches,
and buds to go on. What can you identify?

I DID IT! DATE:

CHAPTER 44

Flowers

Searching for flowers can often feel like a treasure hunt—several flowers are extremely rare and only bloom for a few weeks a year. Indeed, spotting a yellow lady's slipper or a yellow fringed orchid can feel as rewarding as taking in a dramatic view or discovering a rushing waterfall, maybe even more so. Learn to identify wildflowers so that you don't hike by one of these rare treasures without realizing it. Knowing their season of bloom, habitat, and appearance will help you find them.

YELLOW LADY'S SLIPPER

YELLOW FRINGED ORCHID

Petals

The color, shape, and number of petals on a flower can help you identify which family or group of flowers it belongs to.

PETAL COLOR ▸ The color of a wildflower is one of the first things that jumps out at you! And perhaps that is why so many guidebooks sort their flower identification based on color. If you find a white wildflower along the trail then you can flip to the grouping of white wildflowers in your field guide and narrow it down from there. The tricky part is that some flowers, such as lady's slippers and violets, can bloom in different colors, so it's helpful to learn a few other ways to categorize and identify flowers as well.

PETAL SHAPE A wheel…bowl…trumpet…Is this a list of random things stored in your attic? Well maybe, but it also describes different shapes of a blooming flower.

ROTATE OR "WHEEL-SHAPED" FLOWER

A rotate bloom looks similar to a flat tray that a waiter might carry in a restaurant. The petals are even with one another and perhaps ever so slightly upturned at the tips, like this geranium.

CRATERIFORM OR "BOWL-SHAPED" FLOWER

A bowl formation looks just like…you guessed it, a bowl! These cupped flowers look like half a sphere with rounded or pointed petal tips as the border. As the bloom matures the bowl may eventually open and flatten out. A cheery yellow example of a bowl-shaped flower is the buttercup.

FUNNELFORM OR "TRUMPET-SHAPED" FLOWER

A trumpet-shaped flower starts with a thin neck and that then bursts open with a wide bloom. You may not get any music out of these flowers if you blow through the back of them, but they are so pretty that they may make your heart sing. The wild petunia is an example of a trumpet-shaped flower.

There are more than just three shapes that describe the blooms of wildflowers. Check out some of the other flower shapes:

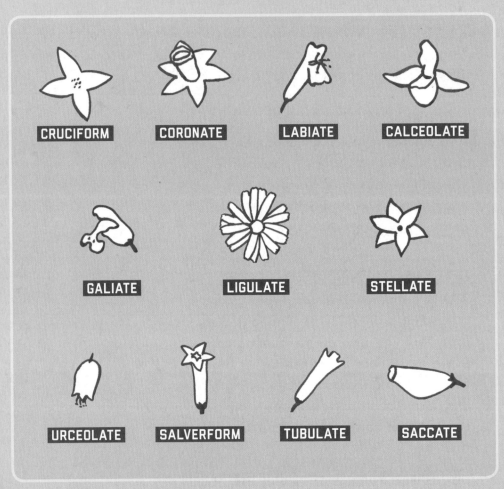

CRUCIFORM

CORONATE

LABIATE

CALCEOLATE

GALIATE

LIGULATE

STELLATE

URCEOLATE

SALVERFORM

TUBULATE

SACCATE

NUMBER OF PETALS There are two main categories of wildflowers: monocots and dicots. Monocots only have one cotyledon—the part of the seed that will eventually grow into leaves. Dicots have two cotyledons. But instead of remembering about cotyledons and what that means, most of the time you can easily identify which of the two categories a wildflower falls into by counting its petals. If it has petals that come in multiples of four or five, meaning that a flower could have four, five, eight, ten, twelve, fifteen, sixteen, or twenty petals...or more, then it is probably a dicot. If the flower has three petals or comes in a multiple of three, then it is most likely a monocot.

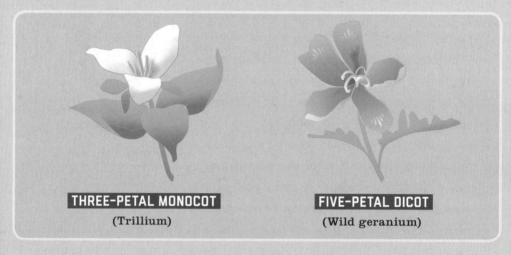

THREE-PETAL MONOCOT
(Trillium)

FIVE-PETAL DICOT
(Wild geranium)

Time of Year

There are a few wildflowers in tropical climates that can bloom year-round, but most flowers have a season. Learning the season when specific flowers bloom will allow you to plan a hike at the right time of year to see them.

The first wildflowers to bloom in a broadleaf forest every year are the spring ephemerals. *Ephemeral* simply means that something is fleeting or exists for a short amount of time. These flowers earn their name because the plants disappear by the heat of summer, when the trees have completely leafed out and shade the forest floor where they grow. Spring ephemerals rely on the sun coming through the leafless branches in late winter to warm the forest floor and activate their growth. They flower for two to three weeks a year and then go dormant, waiting another fifty weeks to bloom again.

Habitat

Habitat characteristics such as elevation and moisture affect bloom times and limit where certain wildflowers grow. These factors can also help you narrow down places and times to search for certain species. Some flowers need ample water to bloom and thrive; others, such as the purple and pink flowers of the prickly pear cactus, can survive with limited moisture. Other wildflowers live only at certain elevations. For example, the alpine false candytuft thrives at higher elevations and cooler western climates. It can usually be found on rocky slopes or above the tree line in Montana, Idaho, and Washington. Sky pilot, true to its name, also grows at high altitudes. Because it takes longer for the ground to warm up (and snow to melt) at higher elevations, flowers in these habitats will generally bloom later than those at lower elevations.

PRICKLY PEAR CACTUS

TRACK IT ↘ Flower Spotting!

Seeing wildflowers is an added bonus on any hike. Whether a blooming cactus in the desert or the state flower wherever you are hiking, it is sure to brighten your day.

➤ Record any flower sightings by sketching the flower using colored pencils. (And if your hiking pace means you've gotta run, you can snap a photo with a camera and use that as a reference later on.)

➤ Make notes to help you identify the flower later using a wildflower guide or the internet.

➤ Write down details like the color of the flower, how many petals it has, and whether or not the stem has fine hairs growing on it.

➤ Don't forget the date because some wildflowers only make a brief appearance. If you go back to find it again, it might be gone!

➤ Taking a picture of the flower can also capture some of the detail that might be difficult to re-create in a drawing.

If you spend time drawing and identifying a flower, then there is a very, very good chance that you will be able to identify the same flower the next time you pass it on the trail.

I SAW A

WHEN
DATE

WHERE
LOCATION,
APPROXIMATE
ELEVATION

NOTES
DESCRIBE
THE
FLOWER

I SAW A

WHEN
DATE

WHERE
LOCATION,
APPROXIMATE
ELEVATION

NOTES
DESCRIBE
THE
FLOWER

TAKE IT TO THE NEXT LEVEL ↗

Latin Names

Most hikers learn the common names of flowers, but if you want to be really precise, learn the Latin names as well. Latin names can be long and sound funny, but if you learn them, you will always know exactly which flower you're looking at. Common names can be confusing—the same plant can have several different common names. For example, trailing arbutus is often called mayflower. It got the name because it was growing around Plymouth, Massachusetts, and gave hope to the Pilgrims after a long winter. Although there might be several common names, there is only one Latin name—in this case, *Epigaea repens*.

CHAPTER 45

Mushrooms

Mushrooms not only look awesome and make you think that tiny gnomes are living along the trail, but they also have incredible abilities. Mushrooms are decomposers—they break down solid waste and dead matter and turn it into nutrients, which feed the producers (plants), which in turn feed the consumers (animals). Mushrooms can also be edible, medicinal, and poisonous. There is a black-and-brown mushroom called chaga that grows on birch trees in forests over 4,000 feet. In Siberia, they use chaga for teas and tonics to treat cancer. On the other hand, a tall, bright white mushroom called angel of death, also known as destroying angel, is highly poisonous and can be potentially deadly if eaten.

CHAGA

ANGEL OF DEATH

When you find a mushroom, don't just identify it based on its appearance. Take time to notice the surroundings of the mushroom as well. Some mushrooms only grow near streams and water while other mushrooms might prefer to make their home at the base of a pine or oak tree. If you learn where mushrooms like to live, they will be easier to find and identify.

Fun Fungus Fact

Hikers often confuse mushrooms and fungus. The truth is all mushrooms are fungi, but not all fungi are mushrooms. Fungi include many other organisms like the yeast we use to bake bread and the mold that grows in the cracks of a shower. Yuck! Mushrooms are actually the fruiting body of certain types of fungi, designed to produce and spread spores for reproduction of the fungus.

There are thousands of different types of mushrooms in North America, and only a small percentage of them are known to be poisonous. With the vast majority, it's simply not known whether they can harm you. However, the fact that *any* mushrooms are poisonous should give you cause for concern if you decide to handle wild mushrooms. Always wear gloves and wash your hands with soap and water when you are finished.

If you are interested in foraging mushrooms, learn to identify them with an experienced mycologist or fungus expert. You can do that by joining a local mycology club. These groups put the "fun" in fungus. They usually offer hikes and workshops focused on mushrooms.

There are lots of different categories of mushrooms, but a good way to get started is to learn three primary groups, which are based on how a mushroom produces and releases the fungus spores for reproduction.

Gilled Mushroom

These are what most people picture when they think of mushrooms. Gilled mushrooms typically have an umbrella-like cap that sits on top of a stem. A series of flaps, or gills, under the cap produce the spores. Here are two common varieties:

MILKY CAP These brown-capped gilled mushrooms grow a few inches off the ground and are easy to distinguish because they drip or leak a milky white substance when their cap is scratched or pierced. If you don't want to touch the mushroom with your fingers, you can use a small twig to pierce the cap and see whether or not it "bleeds" a white liquid. It also leaves your fingers smelling bitter. Be warned: That milky white substance smells like fish, so try not to handle these mushrooms too much or you may end up smelling like cod!

OYSTER Oyster mushrooms range in color from white to light brown. Their gills run directly down the stem in a fan shape, but their caps appear to look like, well . . . an oyster. These mushrooms tend to grow on dead or dying broadleaf wood, particularly the decaying trunks of beech or aspen trees.

Polypores

If a mushroom is growing on a tree or log and feels hard or like cork, then it is a polypore. Polypores come in many different forms, but all have hundreds of tiny pores that discharge fungus spores. Some polypores look like shelves growing out of the wood, and are often called shelf fungi. Others appear to be covered in hair, such as the lion's mane mushroom. These two polypore mushrooms are commonly found in North American woods:

REISHI Reishi mushrooms are prized around the world for their medicinal qualities. They have been credited with boosting immunity and combating fatigue and depression. There are different types of reishi, but the most common medicinal variety is harvested from maple and oak trees. Reishi mushrooms are shiny and shaped like fans. They boast a color range of red, orange, yellow, and white—with the deepest and darkest colors nearest the trunk. They look as if someone has coated them with a glaze or lacquer.

CHICKEN OF THE WOODS This bright orange shelf mushroom is one of the most heavily foraged edible mushrooms. Just as its name suggests, you can cook it in many of the same ways that you would cook chicken meat. Just make sure not to confuse it with another bright orange fungus, the poisonous jack-o'-lantern mushroom. You can tell the difference because the jack-o'-lantern is a gilled mushroom, not a polypore. The gills of a jack-o'-lantern mushroom will also give off a slight green glow in the dark. How freaky (and cool) is that?!

JACK-O'-LANTERN

CHICKEN OF THE WOOD

Boletes

Boletes look like gilled mushrooms, with caps and stems, but instead of gills underneath the cap, a bolete will look as if it has spongy foam. This "foam" is actually a collection of tightly packed tubes that release the fungus spores. The tubes can be so dense that you can hardly see the holes. Here is a common bolete:

PORCINI The nutty taste of this brown mushroom makes it a popular addition to pasta. These thick-stemmed mushrooms pop up in the fall and summer on the ground near trees with needles such as pine, hemlock, and spruce.

TRY IT → Making Spore Prints

Making a spore print is a great way to identify mushrooms and make some cool art for your refrigerator—or wherever you like to hang your artwork. Some people even use their spore prints to cultivate and grow mushrooms at home.

WHAT YOU'LL NEED

➣ Gloves, a couple of gilled mushrooms, white paper, and a glass bowl.

STEP 1 Wearing your gloves, gather a few gilled mushrooms, such as a milky cap.

STEP 2 Cut the stalk of the mushroom right below the gills.

STEP 3 Place the mushroom on the white paper and cover it with a glass bowl.

STEP 4 Wait six to twelve hours. (That's the hard part!)

STEP 5 Remove the bowl and carefully lift the mushroom cap off the paper to reveal the spore print.

Some mushrooms release black, dark brown, tan, white, pink, orange, or green spores. Can you use the shape of the mushroom and the color of the spore print to identify what type of mushroom it is?

I DID IT! DATE:

TRACK IT ↘ Mushroom Spotting!

We're going on a mushroom hunt!
Mushrooms can be very fun to spot in the
woods. With a variety of sizes, colors, and
types, you never know what you will find
growing on a log or nestled up against
the base of a tree. Remember to look,
but not touch, as you take notes.

I SAW A

WHEN
DATE

WHERE

IS THE AREA WET OR DRY?

SUNNY OR SHADY?

IS IT GROWING NEAR A TREE?
WHAT KIND OF TREE?

WHAT COLOR IS IT?

NOTES

I SAW A

WHEN
DATE

WHERE

IS THE AREA WET OR DRY?

SUNNY OR SHADY?

IS IT GROWING NEAR A TREE?
WHAT KIND OF TREE?

WHAT COLOR IS IT?

NOTES

I DID IT! DATE:

TAKE IT
TO THE **NEXT LEVEL** ↗

Homegrown Mushrooms

You can grow your own mushrooms at home! Find a log, drill holes into it, and then fill the holes with mushroom plugs or sawdust spawn, which are presaturated with fungus that will grow mushrooms. (You can order mushroom plugs and sawdust spawn online and pick the exact type of mushrooms that you want to grow.) Once you've filled the holes, cover them with wax (also available online and in most home mushroom kits). Place the log in a shady and moist area near your house. Now watch them grow!

I DID IT! DATE:

ROCKS
AND
GEOLOGY

CHAPTER 46

Different Types of Rocks

We walk beside and over rocks all the time without thinking too much about them. Yet all rocks tell a story. Some rocks show us how old a place is or how the area was formed, and other rocks can tell us what the earth beneath us is made of and who lived here before us. Rocks can even illustrate the movement of water over hundreds of thousands of years. The study of these stories in the solid earth is called geology.

The rocks that surround us are divided into three main types based on how they were formed: igneous, sedimentary, and metamorphic. Knowing the characteristics of these three main categories will help you identify the different types of rocks on your next hike, and it will teach you how the earth beneath your feet was formed.

Igneous

Igneous rock is formed by molten earth that cools and becomes hard. If melted earth sounds weird (because it totally does), then think of it like chocolate—a solid substance that can be hard, but softens when heated up. Similarly, the extremely high temperatures deep below the earth's surface, in the mantle, liquefy rock, turning it into magma. This magma is sometimes pushed up to the earth's surface when a volcano erupts, releasing lava.

When lava cools, it becomes igneous rock. But often the magma remains trapped below the earth's surface and cools over thousands of years; this, too, creates igneous rock. Two types of igneous rock are obsidian and granite:

OBSIDIAN ▶ Obsidian is formed when lava above the earth's surface cools very quickly and creates a dark black glass. It looks like a shiny piece of coal.

GRANITE ▶ Granite is formed when magma cools beneath the earth's surface. It has grains and crystals that are visible to the naked eye—and, when cut and polished, make a nice-looking kitchen countertop. Did you know that Mount Rushmore is also made of granite?

GEODES

When magma cools, trapped gases create hollow bubbles in the igneous rock. Mineral-rich water seeps through these cavities, leaving tiny crystals clinging to the sides of the bubble. Over millions of years, the flow of water in and out builds up the crystals to create a geode. Geodes look like a rough and ordinary rock from the outside, but when you crack them open, they reveal a stunning display of beautiful crystals.

Sedimentary

Have you ever eaten a kitchen sink cookie? These cookies earn their name because bakers put "everything but the kitchen sink" into the cookie batter—you might take a bite and find raisins, chocolate chips, cranberries, caramel, marshmallows, butterscotch, or pecans. Well, sedimentary rock is the kitchen sink cookie of geology.

Sedimentary rocks contain a lot of different ingredients—shells, bones, plants, pebbles—whatever happened to be around when water deposited eroded particles from other rocks in an area. As more and more sediment was deposited over time, the pressure compacted and cemented the layers into sedimentary rock, preserving evidence of whatever was buried. So sedimentary rocks can tell us about the history of a place. For example a sedimentary rock may contain evidence of aquatic plants and animals, telling us that the place where we live was once completely underwater! Generally only sedimentary rocks contain these fossils of past plant and animal life. So the next time you find sedimentary rock, look for imprints, tracks, and bones from hundreds or thousands of years ago. Sandstone and coal are sedimentary:

SANDSTONE ▶ Sandstone, as the name suggests, is a hard rock made of fine grains of sand. The grains are most often quartz and feldspar, which are both tough and weather-resistant minerals. The red and orange sandstone formations in the southwestern United States, such as Arizona's famous Wave and slot canyons, make for some of the most scenic hikes in the country.

COAL Coal is a sedimentary rock that is actually formed from plant debris. It is the product of plants that died in swamps but did not fully decay under the layers of mud. Over millions of years, heat and pressure compressed the layers of organic matter into coal. Isn't it neat to think that green stems and leaves can turn into hardened black rocks?! And yes, this is the type of coal that is burned to produce energy to power things like old-time steam engines and electricity plants. But don't confuse it with the charcoal we use for a summer cookout. Charcoal is made from the coals of burned wood and is not a sedimentary rock.

THE GOLDEN DOORSTOP

Over two hundred years ago a twelve-year-old boy was taking a walk by a rushing creek on a sunny spring day in North Carolina. He started to get hot from walking, so he decided to sit down and soak his feet in the cold water. As he sat on the bank he noticed something shiny underwater. He stood up and took a few steps closer, plunged his hands into the water, and picked up a super-heavy, shiny rock that was the size of a loaf of bread. The boy thought the rock he'd found was pretty—and so did his parents—so the family used it as a doorstop. It was years before they realized that the doorstop was actually a huge gold nugget!

Metamorphic

Metamorphic rocks are rocks that were once igneous or sedimentary but were altered by extreme heat or pressure. Really extreme, as in earthshaking. The plates that make up the earth's crust shifted, increasing the temperature and pressure on existing rocks so much that their mineral compositions changed. Marble and slate are both metamorphic:

MARBLE Marble started off as the sedimentary rock limestone, which was recrystallized and made more dense. If you are looking for examples of marble, then it's a bit disappointing to learn that the round marbles you play with are made of glass. However, you can find it in fancy kitchens or bathrooms and the entire Taj Mahal, which is a famously beautiful marble building in India.

SLATE Slate was created from sedimentary rocks like shale and mudstone that were once clay. Slate readily splits into thin sheets, and a pile of slate often resembles a stack of papers, but in rock form. Slate is used for walkways and roofs and other building materials that need to be thin, strong, and flat.

Making Fossils

WHAT YOU'LL NEED

➢ Leaves or other parts of plants, and soft dough or modeling clay.

STEP 1 Collect plants or leaves. Try to find ones that have already fallen off so you are not damaging a living plant.

STEP 2 Once you get home, press these items into soft dough or modeling clay.

STEP 3 Allow the dough or clay to heat up and dry out in the sun for a few days.

STEP 4 Remove any plants or leaves that remain on the hardened clay.

The impressions that remain are now fossils for you to keep!

I DID IT! DATE:

TRACK IT → Rock Spotting!

The next time you take a hike, look for cool
rocks along the trail. Depending on the
type of rock and the place you are hiking,
you may need to sketch it and leave the
rock there for others to enjoy. But if you
are playing in a streambed, with hundreds of
smooth multicolored rocks, then it is probably
okay to take one home. Either way, try to identify the rock
by searching the internet or visiting a local rock shop to
see whether they can help you identify the rocks you find.

I SAW A ▸

WHEN ▸
DATE

WHERE ▸
BE SPECIFIC

SIZE ▸

☐ ROUGH   ☐ SMOOTH   ☐ SEDIMENTARY   ☐ IGNEOUS   ☐ METAMORPHIC

NOTES ▸

I DID IT! DATE:

I SAW A

WHEN
DATE

WHERE
BE SPECIFIC

SIZE

☐ ROUGH ☐ SMOOTH ☐ SEDIMENTARY ☐ IGNEOUS ☐ METAMORPHIC

NOTES

I SAW A

WHEN
DATE

WHERE
BE SPECIFIC

SIZE

☐ ROUGH ☐ SMOOTH ☐ SEDIMENTARY ☐ IGNEOUS ☐ METAMORPHIC

NOTES

I SAW A

WHEN
DATE

WHERE
BE SPECIFIC

SIZE

☐ ROUGH ☐ SMOOTH   ☐ SEDIMENTARY ☐ IGNEOUS ☐ METAMORPHIC

NOTES

I SAW A

WHEN
DATE

WHERE
BE SPECIFIC

SIZE

☐ ROUGH ☐ SMOOTH   ☐ SEDIMENTARY ☐ IGNEOUS ☐ METAMORPHIC

NOTES

CHAPTER 47

Rock Formations

You may not realize it, but nearly every landform that you pass on a trail is a rock formation—all mountains and valleys, and even the ocean floor, are rises and depressions within the earth's rocky crust. But certain rock formations can often be the destination or the highlight of your hike. Take in a panorama from atop a mesa, marvel at a boulder that seems to have come from nowhere, play hide-and-seek amid desert hoodoos, or walk under a natural arch. You can research the geology of your region online or in regional field guides to find the special rock features near where you live.

GORGES OR CANYONS The terms *gorge* and *canyon* are interchangeable when it comes to rock formations. They are both a deep valley with sheer cliffs on either side. And they are both carved out by the consistent wear of water over an extended period of time. It's incredible to think that a constant stream of water can actually carve a gorge deep into the earth, but the constant flow of water over time carries away rocks and sediment, deepening the channel of the river or stream. In places where the earth's crust is made of sedimentary rocks such as sandstone, the canyon will form in a shorter amount of time and the results can be extra impressive. Like at the Grand Canyon in Arizona.

BUTTES A butte (pronounced like *beaut* as opposed to *but*) looks like a tall cake placed on a flat surface. It is an isolated hill or mountain with sheer sides and a flat top. One of the most photographed buttes is Devils Tower in Wyoming.

MESAS A mesa is very similar to a butte but much larger. *Mesa* means "table" in Spanish, and they do look like flat tables sitting on the earth's surface. Mesas and buttes are both formed when the softer rock surrounding them erodes away, leaving a rock formation with a relatively flat top. One of the most famous mesas in the United States is Mesa Verde in Colorado. The national park preserves the structures of the Ancestral Pueblo people who built homes and whole villages underneath overhanging cliffs while they farmed the mesa top.

ARCHES AND BRIDGES Like mesas and buttes, a natural arch or bridge is formed when softer rock erodes away. A bridge is formed when running water forces its way through the rock over time. Arches are formed when rain seeps into porous rock and dissolves some of the minerals holding it together. If you want to see several arches in one day then check out Arches National Park in Utah, where you can spend days hiking to and through its natural red gateways.

HOODOOS ▸ Although these rock features sound like candy that comes out for Halloween, hoodoos are actually thin rock spires that stand up like the candles on top of a cake. (It all still ties back to cake!) You may have made hoodoo-like creations when you built drip castles at the beach, but these rock formations are not created by stacking or building. Like buttes and arches, these thin towers are revealed when the surrounding dirt and rock erodes away. Utah's Bryce Canyon National Park contains the most well-known collection of hoodoos in the United States.

GLACIAL ERRATIC ▸ Have you ever discovered a huge boulder about the size of a house that is sitting by itself—as though it fell from the sky? Chances are that you have discovered a glacial erratic, a large rock that was pushed away from its initial location by a glacier, which is an enormous, slow-moving sheet of ice. These lonely rocks are always a fun discovery on the trail. And if you find a bunch of them in a field, it is a great place for a quick game of hide-and-seek. Yellowstone National Park has a famous one called the Glacier Boulder.

TRACK IT ↘

Spotting Rock Formations

Be a geologist on your next hike and try to identify different rock formations by sketching any you see along the trail. If you can immediately identify the rock formation, then go ahead and label your sketch. Otherwise, do an online search or check out a book at your local library to see if you can identify the rock formation. You might even want to see if there is a unique formation nearby and make that a destination on your next hike.

I DID IT! DATE:

I SAW A

WHEN
DATE

WHERE
BE SPECIFIC

NOTES

I SAW A

WHEN
DATE

WHERE
BE SPECIFIC

NOTES

I SAW A

WHEN
DATE

WHERE
BE SPECIFIC

NOTES

I SAW A

WHEN
DATE

WHERE
BE SPECIFIC

NOTES

I SAW A

WHEN
DATE

WHERE
BE SPECIFIC

NOTES

PART V

SURVIVAL

What would
YOU do?

You are hiking with your family,

but your little sister is going slow and you decide to run ahead. After fifteen minutes you stop and eat a snack to wait for the rest of your family. You wait and wait and wait. Twenty minutes pass by, and it feels like an eternity. You start to worry and you decide to hike back toward your family. After a few minutes you come to a trail crossing that you don't remember from before. The paths go in four different directions, and you're not sure which trail your family took. What would you do?

SAFETY

AND

FIRST AID

CHAPTER 48

Blisters

Hopefully a blister is the worst injury you ever have to deal with. Blisters are fluid-filled bubbles under the skin. They are most often caused by rubbing or friction. If you hike long enough—or, potentially, if you hike just a little bit—then you will have to learn how to deal with blisters. Knowing how to prevent, treat, and care for blisters will not only keep you more comfortable on the trail, but it will also prevent infection and limit pain that could otherwise end your hike. You might be surprised at just how bad a blister can hurt!

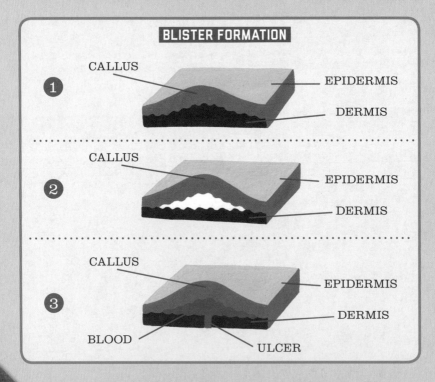

BLISTER FORMATION

1 CALLUS EPIDERMIS DERMIS

2 CALLUS EPIDERMIS DERMIS

3 CALLUS EPIDERMIS DERMIS BLOOD ULCER

Prevention

To prevent blisters, start walking and getting in shape before going on a long and challenging hike. Walking daily or taking short hikes will help toughen up some of the skin on your feet. That tough skin serves as a natural bandage and delays the onset of blisters. So if you're a pedicure person, paint your toenails all kinds of pretty, but leave your lizard layer.

Another important step is to break in your hiking shoes or boots before you hit the trail. Wearing new sneakers or boots on a hike is usually a recipe for disaster. Spend time walking around the house and then around the neighborhood in a new pair of hiking shoes so that by the time you hit the trail, your shoes are more flexible and better molded to your feet.

Most of the time, before a full-fledged blister pops up, hikers will experience a "hot spot." A hot spot feels like…like…like…a hot spot. There is burning and a little bit of pain. Do not try to push through the pain! As soon as you feel a hot spot, sit down, take off your shoe, and apply a barrier such as moleskin, an adhesive bandage, or a patch of wool to the area. Some hikers even like to cover it with duct tape or superglue. No matter what you use, the most important thing is to take care of the hot spot as soon as it is detected. If you walk through a hot spot, it will blister very quickly.

I DECIDED TO HOP ON ONE FOOT INSTEAD OF TREATING MY BLISTER!

Treatment

Once you have a blister, treat it as soon as possible to prevent it from becoming bigger and more painful.

If the blister looks flat, then clean it, bandage it, and keep walking. If it's bigger than your adhesive bandages, use gauze and tape so that no adhesive touches the blister. Adhesive will rip the fragile skin when you try to take it off.

Keeping the skin intact is the best bet to prevent infection, but if the blister becomes too painful to keep walking or bubbles up so much that it looks like it will pop on its own, then you'll need to drain it. Once you've got your shoes and socks off, thoroughly rub your hands with hand sanitizer for twenty seconds, then wipe the blistered area with an alcohol pad. (If you are doing this for a fellow hiker, wear gloves.)
The best way to drain a blister is to use a sterilized sewing needle or safety pin. Remember to include one in your first aid kit. You can sterilize the needle by wiping it down with an alcohol pad or holding it in a flame from a lighter until the needle is glowing red hot. You'll need to wipe off any residue with gauze.

When everything is clean, use the needle to puncture the blister in several places around the edges. Don't go too deep or fast with the needle—only poke until you feel a small release. Allow the fluid to drain out, leaving the top layer of skin in place (pressure is not needed or recommended). After the liquid has drained, apply an

ointment and cover the area with gauze, making sure you tape it well away from the fragile skin. Keep the area clean and check the blister every day for signs of infection—it's draining yellow or green pus, or the area around the blister is red, swollen, warm, or very painful.

Blood Blisters

Most blisters are filled with clear liquid, but occasionally you may get a red blister. Don't panic! Red, or even purple, bubbles of fluid are most likely just blood blisters, especially if they appear in the same areas that regular blisters do. Blood blisters should be bandaged and kept clean like regular blisters, but you should only drain them if they are excessively large. (If they pop on their own, be sure to clean and disinfect them, leaving the top layer of skin in place.) Blood blisters can also develop under your toenails; the larger they grow, the more likely you are to lose your toenail! But if you have to say goodbye to your toenail, it will eventually grow back.

TRY IT → Draining a Balloon Blister

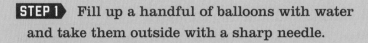

WHAT YOU'LL NEED

➤ A couple of balloons, water, and a sewing needle or safety pin.

STEP 1 Fill up a handful of balloons with water and take them outside with a sharp needle.

STEP 2 One of the best ways to practice piercing a blister is to practice on a water balloon. The more gentle you are, the less likely the water balloon is to pop. Be as careful as possible and pierce the balloons as many times as you can before they either release their water like a sprinkler or pop in your hands!

STEP 3 Pick up any pieces of broken balloons and throw them away. If you have a few extra balloons, consider staging a sneak attack on a sibling or friend.

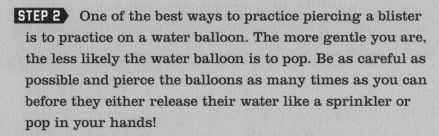

I DID IT! DATE:

CHAPTER 49

Open Wounds

A minor cut or scrape on the trail can be easily cleaned and bandaged in a way that will allow most hikers to continue on their hike. Deep cuts and large abrasions will still need to be cleaned and bandaged on the trail, but they are also a reason to stop your hike and take the shortest route to a place where you can seek the medical attention of a doctor.

Minor Cuts and Scrapes

If you hike enough, you will get a few scrapes on the trail. Maybe you have to push through a briar patch to get to a water source and you end up with cuts on your legs. Maybe your pack doesn't fit well, and it rubs some of the skin off your collarbone. Regardless of how and when you experience these minor cuts and abrasions, stop and take care of them right away. Small injuries that are ignored can easily turn into much bigger problems when you are in the woods. It's not exactly a sanitary environment!

Dirt on your skin and gear can easily enter a wound and cause infection. What you thought was just a simple scrape could painfully cut your trip short. So if you get a cut or scratch, take the time to stop and tend to it.

Before you treat any wound, large or small, always remember to clean your hands by rubbing them thoroughly with sanitizer for twenty seconds and to wear gloves to prevent infection. For minor cuts and scrapes, rinse the affected area with clean water and pat it dry with gauze. (Use antiseptic wipes if you don't have enough clean water to spare.) Cover the area with salve and a bandage to keep out dirt. Be alert for signs of infection such as redness, warmth, swelling around the area, or increasing pain.

Major Cuts and Abrasions

Even though hiking is not a contact sport and backpacking isn't fast paced, deep cuts and large abrasions can happen. If you are whittling a hiking stick at your campsite with a dull pocket knife or maybe even cutting a block of cheese and not paying attention, then you could get a deep cut. Maybe you are trying to go over a tree that has fallen across the trail and a branch is sticking out and it rips open the skin on your leg. And walking on ice or snow, or across slippery rocks can all cause substantial abrasions if you fall.

Your first priority in treating major cuts and abrasions is to stop the bleeding. Elevate the wound if possible and cover the area with gauze or clean cloth. Apply constant pressure for at least ten minutes. Once the bleeding has stopped, you'll need to clean the wound to prevent infection. For this you'll need clean water and a syringe. Most first aid kits include a syringe. To clean a deep cut, fill the syringe with clean water and flush out the impacted area. Flushing isn't overly complicated; it just means using the syringe to force a stream of water into the cut to wash out any dirt and debris.

After flushing the wound with water, dry the area with sterile gauze, apply ointment to keep the wound moist, and cover it with gauze and adhesive tape. Apply pressure by wrapping the bandage tightly all the way around the limb.

For example, if you have a deep cut on your shin, place a bandage on it and then put medical tape over the bandage and wrap it around your calf several times with a tight fit. If you don't have tape, you can use an extra hiking shirt or bandanna to wrap the cut tightly.

A major injury means an immediate evacuation from the trail. Often if people are injured, they are not thinking clearly, so after cleaning and bandaging the wound, take a deep breath and maybe even grab a snack or some water as you look at your maps and guidebooks to decide the best and quickest way to get off trail and to a doctor.

Responding to a Deep Cut

STEP 1 Send your friend outside with a red marker and some fake blood or ketchup if you are feeling gross and creative. Tell her to draw a wound somewhere on her exposed skin and make it look as disgusting as she would like with any extra makeup or condiments available.

STEP 2 After five minutes, head outside to find your friend. When you see her, ask her what happened and then start helping her take care of the wound. If there are gloves in your first aid kit, use them!

STEP 3 Use gauze and pressure to stop the bleeding. Feel free to squirt more ketchup on your skin to depict more blood (and because it's fun).

STEP 4 Practice flushing out the wound with a syringe and clean water. (This might get red on some clothing, but it should all come out in the laundry.)

STEP 5 Bandage the wound with tape, a wrap, an extra piece of clothing, or your hand.

STEP 6 Ask your friend how she thinks you did helping her treat her wound. Is there something you would do differently next time?

STEP 7 Swap roles with your partner and run through steps 1–6 again. Hopefully, it will be easier for both of you the second go-round.

STEP 8 Remember to wipe all the fake blood off your skin before going back into the house so that your family doesn't flip out when they see you!

I DID IT! DATE:

TRACK IT ↘

Using Visualization for Emergencies

Did you know that visualizing an action can help you handle a similar situation in real life? Elite athletes use visualization to excel in their sports—and you can do the same for emergencies.

➣ First, recall an emergency where you helped out. Did you know how to respond? Would you do anything differently if you were in a similar situation again? Visualize what you would do differently and write it down, step-by-step.

➣ Or, if you've never been in an emergency, think about how you would care for a serious cut while you are on the trail.

What would you do? Think through the steps and write them down. Any other emergencies loom large in your imagination? Prep yourself through visualization.

> **STEP 1**

> **STEP 2**

> **STEP 3**

⬤ **I DID IT!** DATE:

TAKE IT TO THE NEXT LEVEL ↗

Wilderness First Aid

A wilderness first aid course can help you become more comfortable and competent treating injuries in the backcountry. Sign up for one of these courses if you start to spend more time in the backcountry and want to be prepared to take care of yourself, your friends, or other hikers who you might come across.

⬤ **I DID IT!** DATE:

CHAPTER 50

Burns

One of the best ways to prevent burns in the backcountry is to not jerk flaming marshmallows out of a fire. Those fiery, charred globs of gooey sugar are responsible for a strikingly large percentage of backcountry burns.

So if you accidentally leave your marshmallow in the fire a little too long, instead of flicking it away from the flames and launching a flaming dessert into a nearby tent, slowly pull it out of the fire and up where you can safely blow it out. Of course, marshmallows aren't the only backpacking burn hazard. Campfires and camp stoves can cause burns if they are not tended properly. Lightning strikes can also cause serious burns.

If your clothes happen to catch fire, stop what you're doing, drop on the ground, cover your face, and roll until the flames are extinguished. With all burns, quickly remove any clothing, jewelry, or belts from the affected area. They can retain heat and deepen the burn, and they will restrict blood flow when the skin begins to swell. Try to cool down burns with cool water or compresses, which will reduce pain and swelling, but don't immerse large areas in water since you could quickly lose body heat.

The care and treatment of a burn will depend on how severe it is. There are three main types: first, second, and third degree.

FIRST-DEGREE BURNS ▶ A first-degree burn can result from something as common as staying out in the sun too long or accidentally touching a hot pot. It usually results in red skin that is painful. There are no blisters or broken skin. Prevent these mild burns by wearing sunscreen and being careful when cooking or starting a fire. Treat first-degree burns by applying a soothing ointment or aloe. Take ibuprofen to reduce the pain if necessary.

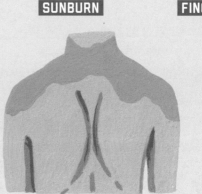

SUNBURN

FINGER BURN

SECOND-DEGREE BURNS ▶ A second-degree burn damages your first and second layers of skin. Skin will be deep red and might be blistered. It may appear wet and shiny and have splotchy white spots. Rinse second-degree burns with clean, cool water and mild soap if you have it, being very careful not to break any blisters, which will protect against infection. Apply a thin layer of antibiotic ointment or aloe to the affected area. Then dress the burn lightly and loosely with sterile, nonstick gauze. Secure the gauze with tape along the edges well away from the burned area so that it doesn't touch any fragile skin. Apply a cold compress to help relieve some of the symptoms.

Many second-degree burns can be cleaned and treated in the backcountry, so you can continue with your trip. Be sure to check for infection and change the dressing once a day. However, if the burn is on the hands or feet, or anywhere near the face, genitals, or armpits, then immediately help the person with the burn to the nearest evacuation point so that he or she can get checked by a doctor. This is also true when there are burns on more than 10 percent of the body. (For a rough gauge, the skin on the back of your hand is about 1 percent of your body.)

THIRD-DEGREE BURNS Third-degree burns are extremely serious as they go down to the innermost layer of skin. They can look white, brown, or black and may have deeply charred skin. The area may feel numb because nerve endings have been destroyed. Third-degree burns require an immediate 911 call and evacuation to the nearest hospital. Refer to chapter 53 for medical response options when there is no cell service. Patients should be wrapped in clean, breathable clothing and given fluids to prevent dehydration.

Natural Cold Compresses

One of the best treatments for first- and second-degree burns is to apply a cold compress, but most hikers don't head out with an ice pack in their first aid kit. However, if it's winter or you're at high elevation where there are snowfields throughout the summer, then fill a ziplock bag full of snow or ice and use that to help cool the burn.

TRY IT →

Sunscreen Experiment

The same ultraviolet rays that cause sunburn can cause colors to fade. See how well sunscreen blocks these rays by testing it out on a piece of construction paper.

WHAT YOU'LL NEED

➤ A dark piece of construction paper (black or navy blue works best), sunscreen, and sunshine.

STEP 1 Fold the construction paper in half. On the left half write WITH SUNSCREEN. On the right half write NO SUNSCREEN.

STEP 2 Lightly spread sunscreen over the half that says WITH SUNSCREEN.

STEP 3 Place the paper outside in the sun and secure it so it won't blow away.

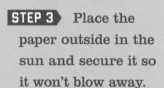

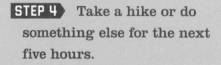

STEP 4 Take a hike or do something else for the next five hours.

STEP 5 After five hours, check on your piece of paper. The half of the page with sunscreen should be much darker than the half without sunscreen.

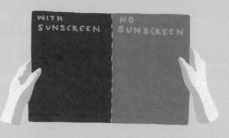

➤ Always protect yourself from first-degree burns and too much sun exposure by putting on sunscreen.

I DID IT! DATE:

TAKE IT TO THE NEXT LEVEL ↗

Natural Remedies

For centuries folk medicine has used plants to help heal and treat burns. These medicinal plants include aloe vera, lavender, comfrey, and plantain. Research the native plants in your area to see whether any of these natural burn remedies—or others—can be found in the wild.

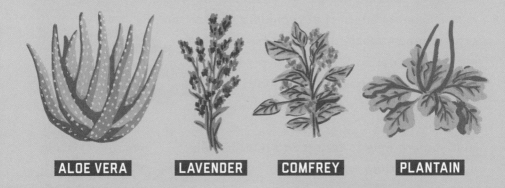

ALOE VERA   **LAVENDER**   **COMFREY**   **PLANTAIN**

I DID IT! DATE:

CHAPTER 51

Twists and Sprains

Unlike deep cuts and severe burns, which happen only rarely in the backcountry, the chances of twisting your ankle or spraining your knee are almost a given after a certain number of hikes. A sprain occurs when you roll or twist a joint in a way that stretches or even tears the tendons and ligaments. If you spend your days stepping on rocks and roots, then eventually your ankles will bend in an unpleasant and painful manner. Oftentimes you can hike through a mild sprain or twist. At other times you'll have to stop and treat it before pressing onward. Occasionally the sprain will be severe enough that you won't be able to continue.

Footwear and Prevention

Reducing the risk of a twisted ankle starts with picking the right pair of shoes. Some hikers believe that high-cut boots are best at providing support and protecting the ankle, but other backpackers insist that wearing a low-cut shoe allows their ankles to gain the strength and flexibility that protects them from twisting their ankle.

If you are new to hiking and tend to twist your ankle, then go with boots. But if you play sports with lots of side-to-side movements and are hiking on a relatively smooth trail, then you are probably fine in low-cut sneakers. No footwear will fully protect you from spraining your ankle, but finding the shoe that's right for you will help.

What to Do When You Sprain Your Ankle...and You Will

When you do sprain your ankle, remember the acronym **RICE**.

R stands for *rest*. Depending on the severity of the sprain, that might mean getting carried out, cutting the hike short, or reducing your miles for the day.

I stands for *ice*. You probably won't have ice cubes in your backpack, but you might be able to collect snow or ice from the trail or stick your leg in a cool creek for relief and to reduce swelling.

C is for *compression*, which limits swelling and restricts potentially more damaging, and painful, movement. How to accomplish this with wrapping and splinting will be discussed on the following pages.

E is for *elevation*, which also helps reduce swelling. If you take a break or are at camp, rest your leg in a comfortable position about the level of your heart. Remember that the ibuprofen in your first aid kit will relieve pain and reduce inflammation, helping hikers hobble along after a sprain.

There are several ways to wrap a sprained ankle, knee, finger, or wrist to limit motion and reduce swelling. If you are wrapping an ankle, keep the foot at a 90-degree angle.

In other words, point your big toe toward your shin when you wrap underneath your foot and around your ankle. The wrap technique for an ankle includes going under the arch of your foot several times like a stirrup and then bringing the brace together by wrapping a figure eight around the foot and ankle.

If you want to further immobilize the joint, you can also add a splint to your wrap. Some hikers carry a soft lightweight splint such a Sam Splint in their first aid kits, but other hikers will fashion a splint with sticks or a hiking pole. If you are using a stiff or uncomfortable object as a splint, cushion it with a shirt or bandage before putting it next to your skin to prevent rubbing. Then wrap the splint to limit motion and provide rigidity.

WHAT YOU'LL NEED

➤ Athletic tape or a cloth ankle wrap such as an ACE bandage.

STEP 1 Take your shoes off. (If you are using athletic tape, either use a medical foam wrap, called a prewrap, to go with it or leave your sock on your foot. If you are using a cloth wrap, take your sock off.)

STEP 2 Point your toe toward your shin and wrap the bandage under the arch of your foot.

STEP 3 Run the bandage across the front of your ankle and then around the back before crossing it over the top middle of your foot and wrapping it back under the arch of your foot. Pull it back up and cross over the tape at the front of your ankle to create an X.

STEP 4 Repeat this motion three times. This is a figure-eight wrapping technique, and it will help provide support, rigidity, and compression to a sprained ankle.

I DID IT! DATE:

Splint Strategies

It's important to know how to wrap and splint your own joints as well as being able to help another injured hiker. Find a friend or sibling and see whether you can practice wrapping their ankle. You can take turns to master your techniques and also practice on other joints such as the knee or wrist.

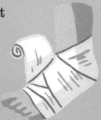

I DID IT! DATE:

CHAPTER 52

Bites and Stings

While the itch of a mosquito bite is annoying and hiking through a patch of stinging nettles is always unpleasant, you don't usually need first aid. However, there are more serious bites and stings that can occur on the trail, and their severity will depend on the circumstances and how your body responds.

Stings from Bees and Other Insects

Bees, wasps, hornets, yellow jackets—there are a wide variety of flying insects with stinging needles attached to their booties. For most folks, a sting here or a few there are not going to lead to anything more than slight pain, isolated swelling or redness, and itching. Treat a sting by cleaning the area around it, removing the stinger fully if needed, and taking a single dose of antihistamine. However, stings become far more serious if they are numerous and cause severe itching and discomfort or if a hiker has an allergic reaction.

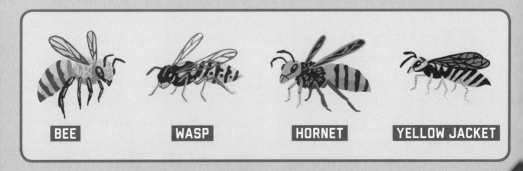

BEE   WASP   HORNET   YELLOW JACKET

Anaphylaxis

Anaphylaxis is a life-threatening allergic reaction. Insect stings are one of the most common triggers of anaphylaxis, and the nuts many hikers carry for food—peanuts and tree nuts like almonds or walnuts—are another common trigger. The symptoms of anaphylaxis include wheezing, trouble breathing, swelling, and hives or a rash all over the body. It can also cause a weak or rapid pulse, dizziness, and vomiting. Anaphylaxis is treated with injected epinephrine. Ask whether the sufferer is carrying an EpiPen and whether they need help to use it. If the sufferer doesn't have an EpiPen, give an antihistamine. In both cases, go as quickly as possible to the nearest medical facility. Even if epinephrine is injected, a second round may be necessary if symptoms persist or return.

If someone suffers anaphylaxis to the point where they are unconscious and not breathing, the next step would be to perform CPR. It is a great life skill to know how to perform CPR (cardiopulmonary resuscitation), especially if you are on the trail and away from immediate medical attention. Wilderness first aid classes offer CPR training, or there are many stand-alone CPR classes offered through the American Red Cross. These courses are affordable and usually take just a few hours to complete. That's a small price to pay to potentially save a life.

Poisonous Plants

Certain plants can also cause allergic reactions and, in rare cases, send you into anaphylaxis. That is one reason to think twice before tromping off trail into unknown shrubbery or using an unidentified leaf when you've run out of toilet paper. And never ingest any plant on the trail unless you are 100 percent certain of its identity and edibility. The most common plants that people have a topical reaction to on the trail are poison ivy, poison sumac, poison oak, and

POISON IVY **POISON SUMAC** **POISON OAK** **STINGING NETTLES**

stinging nettles. Learn what those plants look like before you leave home!

If you do have a reaction to a plant, keep the area clean and treat it with corticosteroid cream or calamine lotion, and take an antihistamine as soon as you can.

Scorpions and Spiders

The first hiker on the trail each morning usually has the unpleasant task of clearing spiderwebs that were built across the path during the night. It is unlikely that you will get a spider bite simply by touching or breaking through a web, but if a spider feels threatened or trapped, then it will sometimes bite as a form of defense. Most spiders and scorpions in the United States are nonvenomous, but a few transmit toxins that can be harmful to humans. Most of the time the symptoms of a scorpion sting or spider bite will stay in one spot and result in swelling and redness. If possible,

apply ice to reduce the inflammation. However, if the symptoms become systemic—meaning that they spread to different parts of your body—then seek immediate medical attention.

Snake Bites

There are lots of people—kids and adults—who are terrified of snakes. However, the likelihood of getting bitten by a snake on the trail is actually extremely low. One way to prevent snake bites is to always examine the surroundings before stopping to take a break and look before placing your hands on a rock. And if it does happen, then there is a good chance that the snake is not venomous. If you do get bit and you can identify the snake with 100 percent certainty and know that it is nonvenomous, then clean the bite and seek medical attention to determine whether or not you need any additional treatment such as a tetanus booster.

However, if there is any uncertainty, or if you know that you were bitten by a venomous snake, then seek immediate medical attention and limit physical activity as much as possible to slow the spread of

RATTLESNAKE

WATER MOCCASSIN

COPPERHEAD

CORAL SNAKE

venom. Admittedly, that can be hard if you are hiking. The group you are with may be able to carry you back to the trailhead. Or, if you are able to call 911 or alert emergency reponse by using a satellite beacon, then a search-and-rescue team will respond and help you evacuate. If you are by yourself or in a small group and without phone or satellite service, then stay calm and hike slowly to a place where you can receive help. Also, remove any jewelry in case of swelling, cover the bite with a loose bandage, and keep the bite below the heart to limit the spread of venom. If you are able to do so safely, get a good look at the snake so you can describe it to the medical professionals who are helping you. If you are able to take a picture from a safe distance, that could also help with identifying the snake. Do not go after the snake or get too close and risk getting a second bite.

If the snake was venomous, there is a chance that its bite was dry, meaning no venom was released. Even if you do hit the unlikely jackpot of being bitten by a snake…that is venomous…and releases its venom…if you are a healthy person and receive prompt medical attention, then you will most likely enjoy a full recovery.

Tick Bites

Instead of being terrified of snake bites, hikers should channel that anxiety into preventing tick bites. Ticks are a major concern on many trails throughout the United States. And while the majority of tick bites are benign or harmless, the tick population has spread, and there has been an increase in tick-borne illnesses—in particular Lyme disease. These illnesses can be very difficult to diagnose.

The best way to prevent a tick-borne disease is to prevent a tick bite. Avoid hiking through tall plants and high grass. You can also tuck

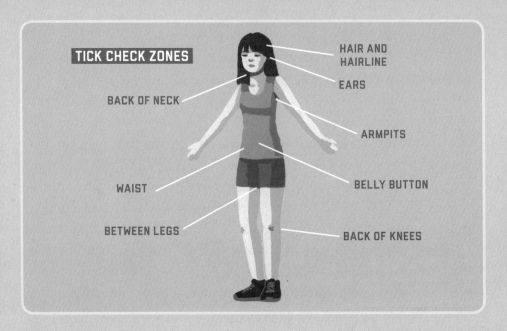

TICK CHECK ZONES

HAIR AND HAIRLINE

EARS

BACK OF NECK

ARMPITS

WAIST

BELLY BUTTON

BETWEEN LEGS

BACK OF KNEES

your shirt into your pants and tuck your pants into your socks to keep ticks off your skin. Ticks are deterred by ample bug spray. You can also treat your gear and clothing with a chemical called permethrin, which will kill ticks on contact. But no matter what prevention you take, also perform frequent tick checks by examining your body and running your hands over any exposed or accessible skin to detect ticks before they embed, or attach.

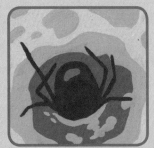

If you do find a tick that is attached to your skin, clean the area with rubbing alcohol. Then, grab the tick by its head with a pair of tweezers and pull the whole tick out. Clean the skin once again with an alcohol pad or soap and water, and monitor the area over the next few days and weeks for any signs of a rash or red circle. If you do experience irritation at the site of the tick bite, or any symptoms of sickness, visit a doctor immediately.

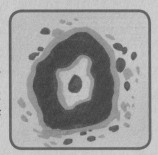

TRY IT → Tick Check

This game will teach you and your friend how to look for a tiny black tick on your own skin as well as others' when you hike.

> **WHAT YOU'LL NEED**
> ➢ A ballpoint pen and a friend.

STEP 1 Ask your friend to cover their eyes. Take a ballpoint pen with black ink and put a dot somewhere on your exposed skin, perhaps on the back of your neck or behind your knee.

STEP 2 Have your friend look for the dot as if it's a tick.

STEP 3 After your dot tick is found, have your friend make a dot for a tick on their skin and see whether you can find it.

I DID IT! DATE:

Poisonous Plants and Animals

Let's face it. Poisonous plants and animals are kinda cool. Especially if you know how to spot them—and hopefully avoid them—on the trail. Research the most common ones in your area and draw one of them below.

I DID IT! DATE:

TAKE IT TO THE **NEXT LEVEL** ↗

Identify Local Dangers

Poisonous plants and dangerous animals are different in different regions of the United States. Do some research to find out what venomous critters and toxic plants might be living in your neck of the woods.

I DID IT! DATE:

CHAPTER 53

Severe Injury

A severe injury on the trail is anything that might require emergency medical attention from first responders. In other words, it requires calling 911. Contacting medical responders from the trail has gotten much easier with increased and improved cell service and new technology such as satellite GPS messengers and beacons.

However, there are still times and places where you will struggle to find service.

If you have several people in your group, then leave the individuals with the greatest medical knowledge with the injured hiker and send another small group to find a clearing or higher ridge where they can get a signal to call or text. Always call 911 directly, because a cell phone without service can often still connect to emergency dispatchers using shared cell towers and signals.

When you talk to the 911 dispatcher, relay as much information as possible, including who is hurt, how they were injured, where the injured hiker is located, and any other medical information such as whether the hiker has asthma or type 1 diabetes. You may be able to read off your exact GPS coordinates to the dispatcher from a smartphone. If you know the nearest access point or trailhead, share that information as well. The dispatcher may be able to give instructions over the phone to help the patient and make the entire group more comfortable and accessible for the search-and-rescue team. If you have any notes on the patient, or other helpful information, have that available. Jot down any instructions you receive from the dispatcher so you can look back at them later.

The initial response to a severe injury on the trail is very similar to the response you would have if you were at home. Make sure the scene is safe, stabilize the injured person, and proceed to treat any injuries to the best of your ability. If there is a chance that there might be a spine injury, encourage the hiker to stay as still as possible, and maybe even hold the hiker's head and neck in a stable position.

The biggest difference between a major medical incident on a hike and one at home is that it could be a long time before the medical crews reach you. Keep everyone in the group—especially the injured hiker—as safe and comfortable as possible. If it is raining and you have tents, set a few of them up. Or if it is hot and sunny, set up shelter for the shade. Make sure everyone is wearing proper clothing for the conditions, and eating and drinking as well.

Most importantly, keep careful watch over the injured hiker. Try to keep them calm and let them know that help is on the way. Continue checking in with the injured hiker to make sure they are alert and ask them if there are any changes in how they feel. If they do report changes in pain or sensation, you should start a SOAP note for the first responders. Taking notes is an important way to record information when someone is injured in the backcountry. SOAP is an acronym that will help you organize notes about the situation in a way that helps medical responders:

SUBJECTIVE Write about what happened from your point of view. What caused the injury? For example, *twenty-year-old man hurt his arm. Main complaint is pain above the wrist.*

OBJECTIVE Record symptoms and information such as a cut that is bleeding or the patient's heart rate.

....

PLAN ▶ State your next steps to address the issues you came across during your assessment. For example, you might stop the bleeding if it is a cut. You could stabilize a fracture. And you could figure out whether the patient needs to leave the backcountry and how that could happen.

Monitor how the injured hiker is doing by checking their pulse every fifteen minutes. You can usually find a heartbeat on the inner wrist or on the neck below the chin, near the carotid artery.

Count how many times the heart beats in a minute and record that as the pulse. Record this along with any other physical changes that you notice or important information given to you by the injured hiker. When first responders arrive, hand them the SOAP note to take with them. It will be very helpful in treating the hiker in the ambulance and at the hospital.

Extra Help

In the aftermath of experiencing, treating, or witnessing a severe injury, remember that traumatic injuries can have emotional and mental impacts, in addition to the physical ones. Checking in with a mental health counselor can help you process and move forward from the event in the best way possible.

 **TRY IT →** **Learning from Others**

WHAT YOU'LL NEED

➢ A couple of older friends—maybe your grandparents or your aunts and uncles— and some time to talk.

STEP 1 Everyone at some point or another has had to treat a personal injury, help someone else, or call 911. Seek out adults you respect and ask them about their experiences. Here are some questions to help get you started:

➢ "Have you ever been seriously injured? What happened and how did you get help?"

➢ "Have you ever needed to help someone who was seriously injured? What did you do? Is there anything you would have done differently?"

STEP 2 Listen to the answers and think about how their experiences can help you better prepare yourself if a serious injury happens to you or another hiker on the trail.

I DID IT! DATE:

Write a SOAP note according to the following scenario:

You're hiking and come across a mountain biker who has fallen off his bike and is holding his knee. He is bleeding from a small cut on the knee, and he says he can't hike or bike or put any pressure on his leg. He seems confused when you start asking questions. You notice a large scratch on his helmet.

➢ Subjective—What happened to the biker?

➢ Objective—What is wrong now?

➢ Assessment—What is your conclusion?

➢ Plan—What is the plan moving forward? If you need to wait for help, is there something you can help the biker with while you wait?

I DID IT! DATE:

CHAPTER 54

Dehydration and Heat-Related Illness

To stay alive, keep hydrated—it's that simple. Most people need about two liters of fluid per day if they are relaxing at home. But your body's needs vary depending on your level of activity, the temperature, and even the altitude. So if you are hiking in hot temperatures, you are probably sweating a lot, which means you are losing a lot of fluid. You should always take more water than you think you need and know where your water sources are along the trail.

Mild Dehydration and Exhaustion

Dehydration is when your fluid loss is more than your intake. You lose water by peeing, pooping, sweating, spitting, crying, and even breathing! (And you can lose water quickly if you suffer from illness such as vomiting or diarrhea. It's never fun to be that kind of sick, especially when you are running for bushes as opposed to a toilet. Be sure to treat water sources to avoid these common symptoms of a waterborne illness.)

You should be able to recognize the signs of dehydration so you can take action immediately:

> **THIRST!**
> Being thirsty is your body's way of
> telling you that you need water.
>
> **DRY MOUTH**   **NO PEE**   **DARK YELLOW PEE**
> **HEADACHE**   **DRY COOL SKIN**   **MUSCLE CRAMPS**

To treat dehydration you need to replace your body's lost fluids. Your body needs both water and electrolytes. If you have a drink mix like Gatorade, you should drink it. Your body needs sugar and salt, so if you have any sweet and salty snacks those will help. The balance of salt and fluids will help your body retain water and regain balance. It will also prevent you from a dangerous health condition known as hyponatremia, which comes from drinking too much water without taking in snacks, sodium, or electrolytes.

Severe Dehydration and Heat Stroke

If someone is experiencing these symptoms they have reached the point of severe dehydration, which can lead to heat stroke, a life-threatening emergency.

SIGNS OF SEVERE DEHYDRATION

→ Feeling dizzy and confused or irritable

→ A rapid heartbeat

→ Very dark urine or no pee

→ Rapid breathing

→ Loss of consciousness

→ Skin might be very dry as the body is no longer able to sweat. At this point, body temperature will rise quickly.

→ Temperatures above 104°F (40°C) impair brain function.

→ Red and hot skin.

→ A rapid heartbeat.

→ Loss of consciousness.

What should you do?

1. If you have cell service, call 911. If you do not have cell signal or a satellite beacon, then send someone from the group—ideally a team of two or more—to find cell service and medical assistance. If this is not possible, continue to step 2.

2. Remove the person from the sun and heat.

3. If the person is suffering from severe dehydration, give them water if they are able to drink. If the person is suffering from heat stroke—with a body temperature of 103°F (39.4°C) or higher—then DO NOT provide water. Instead, cool them down! If you have water, soak a bandanna, shirt, or other clothing item and place it under their armpits and on their neck and groin.

4. Get them to the hospital as quickly as possible.

Dehydration and heat stroke are different, but they are both very serious concerns. However, if you plan ahead, stay hydrated, and avoid hiking in direct sun or walking through the hottest parts of the day, these conditions can usually be avoided.

TRY IT → Hydration Check

On your next hike, pay attention to how often and how much water you drink. Also note how you felt and look at the color of your urine throughout the day and at the end of the day.

➢ If your urine is dark, you know you need to drink more water.

➢ If it is a pale yellow, then you are on track for staying hydrated.

1	
2	HYDRATED
3	
4	
5	DEHYDRATED
6	
7	SEVERELY
8	DEHYDRATED

I DID IT!   DATE:

CHAPTER 55

How to Survive Cold

Winter hiking is just the remedy for those dark, cold days when you're stuck inside all the time. The ground is covered in white, and there is a peaceful feeling as the snow falls silently through the sky. You can look for animal tracks as you walk through the snow-covered pines. If you take the proper gear and do some planning, winter hiking can be just as comfortable as hiking in any other season.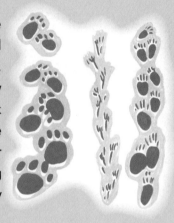

But weather will change quickly and dramatically in winter—especially as you go up in elevation. You might have a sudden snowstorm or a blizzard with high winds or even a whiteout. In whiteout conditions, it is almost impossible to see or navigate because everything seems white! The snow is white, and the sky looks white because of snow and fog. Whiteout conditions are incredibly dangerous because it is easy to get lost. Not to mention the harsh, cold surroundings!

It is a good idea to look at the weather forecast anytime you go hiking, but it is a step

that should never be skipped in the winter. Remember that it will be colder the higher up you go and that sometimes tall peaks have their own weather systems and patterns. If there is a chance you could face low temperatures, don't skimp on the gear you take.

This is what you need to know to survive in the cold:

→ Drink plenty of water. You can get dehydrated in any type of weather if you forget to drink, especially on a cold weather hike. Your body is exerting a lot of energy just keeping warm, and it is still losing water through sweat—especially if you are trekking through snow.

→ Bring plenty of snacks and keep them accessible. Your body needs fuel to stay warm. Keep food in your hip belt or jacket pockets, where you can grab it and eat on the go. Chances are you will be too cold to stop moving.

→ Dress in layers and bring a hat and mittens. If you are climbing a mountain and you start your hike in all your layers, you will be in trouble. The higher you go, the cooler it will be. While you are climbing you might warm up, so shed a layer before you get sweaty. Once you are wet, it will be difficult to stay warm. Wear mittens. Once your fingers get cold, it will be tough to do simple tasks like unbuckle your hip belt, tie your shoes, or pitch your tent. So be sure to put on your hat and mittens before your fingers start to feel cold.

→ Hike during the warmest part of the day. When the sun begins to set in the evening, it will get cold fast. Aim to get to camp and set up before the sun drops behind the mountains and you lose that precious heat.

→ Bring extra socks. You don't want to have cold, wet feet for long. Not only is it uncomfortable, but you risk getting frostbite. It is always good to have a warm, dry pair of socks to sleep in at night.

→ Bring along oven bags or grocery bags to put over your feet. If you will be walking through wet snow or mud, place one of these bags over each foot before you put your shoes on. This will keep your socks and feet dry and hold in some of the warmth.

→ Don't let your shoes freeze overnight. If you are camping in below-freezing temperatures and your shoes are wet, they could be as hard as a rock in the morning. It is extremely difficult to get your feet in frozen shoes! Untie your laces and open the shoe as wide as you can. Put your shoes in a plastic bag and keep them inside your tent, or better yet, put the shoe bag in the foot box of your sleeping bag. If you don't want do this (or if you forget), sit on your shoes the next morning until they thaw out enough for you to put them on.

→ Sleep with the clothes you plan on wearing the next day. One of the worst things about getting dressed on a cold winter morning is putting on freezing clothes. If you don't want to wear them, put your clothes for the next day in your sleeping bag with you. If you don't want them in your sleeping bag, you can keep them between your sleeping bag and sleeping pad. That way you will lie on them all night and they should be warm in the morning.

> → Bring a few packages of hand warmers to pop open and stick inside your gloves when you just can't seem to warm up your hands. They are long lasting and will hopefully be warm long enough for you to set up camp without too much discomfort.
>
> → Be sure you have proper traction devices and equipment if necessary.

Hypothermia

Hypothermia occurs when a person's core body temperature drops to a level where brain and muscle function are impaired. Hypothermia can be life threatening if nothing is done. Use a buddy system in the winter. While recognizing the signs of hypothermia in someone else might be simple, you can rarely spot those signs in yourself. Once the body starts losing more heat than it makes, symptoms of hypothermia begin. The first thing you might notice is that you are cold! In fact, when the body starts to shiver, it is trying to warm itself up. You might also be irritable and begin to complain about almost anything. Pay attention to these initial warnings!

As your body temperature drops, you lose coordination and judgment. It becomes more difficult to do simple things because you lose fine motor control. As you get colder and start shivering harder, you begin to trip and fall. Your skin might turn gray, and you will curl up to try to stay warm.

The *umbles* is a well-known term in the outdoor world, and it will help you remember what to watch out for. Someone with hypothermia might grumble, mumble, fumble, stumble, tumble, and crumble.

GRUMBLE

MUMBLE

FUMBLE

STUMBLE

TUMBLE

CRUMBLE

Eventually a person will lose the ability to talk and their heart rate will drop so low that it will be difficult to find a pulse. This is an emergency situation, so call 911.

While you are waiting for help to arrive, keep the hypothermic hiker from losing heat and help them create more heat. What is one of the most effective ways to generate heat? Eating! If the person is conscious and able to eat, get that started quickly. Once the person is eating, get them warm and dry. Find a safe place out of the wind and rain, take off any wet clothing, and find a way to insulate the body. If you have a sleeping pad or emergency blanket, put them on that instead of the ground. Use whatever items you have—dry clothes, sleeping bag, sleeping bag liner. The ground is cold, and a person can lose a lot of heat sitting directly on it. You can put the hiker in a tent or use a tarp to protect them from the elements.

Frostbite

Frostbite is another concern in cold weather. It occurs when skin and the tissue underneath freeze, literally! Your fingers, toes, nose, ears, cheeks, and chin are most at risk. The first sign of frostbite is cold, red, painful skin, followed by a prickling feeling as the area goes numb. As frostbite progresses the skin will become hard and waxy looking and may turn white or gray.

Frostbite can be very painful and can result in the loss of a finger, toe, or any area that has not been treated early. Like burns, the severity of frostbite depends on how deep the damage goes. It has three stages—frostnip, superficial frostbite, and deep frostbite. At the superficial stage, your skin may actually start to feel warm before it turns numb again as the damage progresses deeper. With deep frostbite, your joints and muscles may no longer work properly.

Superficial and deep frostbite must be treated by a doctor, but you can prevent frostbite from getting that far by stopping when you feel tingling or numbness, and warming the area with skin-to-skin contact. If your fingers are feeling numb or tingly, take your gloves off and place your hands under your layers so that they are touching the skin on your belly, armpits, or even your thighs. If you are layered properly and have been moving, your torso should be a toasty 90°F (32.2°C) or more. Whatever you do, don't rub the skin. That can cause more damage if ice crystals have begun to form.

If the skin is hard and waxy, it is already frostbitten. If there's any chance that the skin will refreeze, do not try to thaw it. Refreezing thawed skin will cause even worse damage. Do not use any direct heat like handwarmers on numb skin because they can cause burns if a person can't feel their skin getting too hot. If you have a stove, heat some water to gently thaw the area. Make sure the water is very warm to the touch, but not hot. You can also sip warm liquids to help warm you from the inside. Rewarming should take about thirty minutes. As the skin thaws, you will feel tingling and burning as blood flow returns. If pain persists or blisters develop, you will need to see a doctor. Be sure to protect the skin from refreezing and do not break any blisters.

If you are out hiking all day in the snow or cold weather and your toes hurt or feel numb, take your shoes off and check your feet! Put on dry socks and put bags over them before your put your shoes back on. People have gone all day outside and taken off their shoes at the end of the day only to find out they have frostbite. At that point the frostbite might be in an advanced stage, and require medical attention.

TRY IT → Human Burrito

Try making a human burrito to warm up a person with hypothermia. Practice this insulation technique with a friend.

> **WHAT YOU'LL NEED**
>
> ➤ An insulating layer (groundsheet or sleeping pad), a sleeping bag, and other items that would be in your backpack on a hike, and a friend or family member.

STEP 1 Put a groundsheet, sleeping pad, or other insulating item on the ground in a safe place.

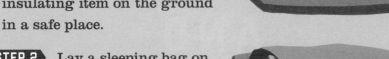

STEP 2 Lay a sleeping bag on top and get the "patient" inside the sleeping bag.

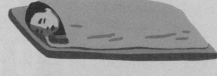

STEP 3 Put as many insulating layers as you have on the patient. For example, if you have a hat, put it on them. (In a real situation on the trail, remember that you can use the items in their bag, too! You can put them in their sleeping bag and put yours over them and tuck it around them.)

STEP 4 Add a layer to protect the patient from the wind and rain.

I DID IT! DATE:

SECTION 2

GETTING LOST... AND FOUND

CHAPTER 56

How to Get Found

Getting lost happens to the very best hikers. And it happens to the very best hikers all the time because they challenge themselves by picking off-the-beaten-path trails that are hard to follow. When you spend some time in nature, getting lost becomes just another part of being outside and exploring. So know how to be found—because getting lost *will* happen.

The most common mistake hikers make when they think they are lost is to panic and make an immediate decision about where to go or what to do. No one wants to feel lost or get left behind by a group, so they rush off trail in the direction that they think they should go.

If you think you might be lost and you are on a trail, *do not* leave the trail. Call out for your group. There is a chance that they are close enough to hear you and respond back. If you don't hear anything after yelling or using an emergency whistle, then take a deep breath. In fact, take a few deep breaths and sit down. Check your cell phone for service if you have one, and call or send a text to your group.

If you try yelling, whistling, and calling on the phone and don't get a response, pull out your water bottle and some food because it's hard to make good decisions when you are hungry and thirsty. It can even be helpful to come up with a positive mantra, an uplifting word or phrase that you repeat over and over again. It could be something simple like "I'm going to be okay" or "I'll be back with my family soon."

Then look at any maps or guidebooks. Look closely at your surroundings. Does anything look familiar? Do you remember any landmarks? Can you see any? Do you see anything that you can identify on the map? If you get to know the place where you are sitting and become familiar with it, then you won't feel as lost. You can get a sense of where you are so you can gain a sense of where to go.

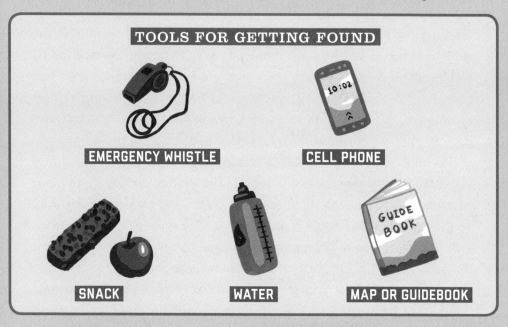

TOOLS FOR GETTING FOUND

EMERGENCY WHISTLE

CELL PHONE

SNACK

WATER

MAP OR GUIDEBOOK

After resting, hydrating, eating, and assessing your location, think about the last time you remember being on the right path or with your group. If you think that you can backtrack on the trail to the correct path, then do that. Turn around and reconnect with the right trail and your group.

But if the trail you are on comes to a junction and you don't know which way to go, **STOP**.

It is always easier to be found staying put where two trails come together than wandering down an unknown path. If at any point you feel confused about which direction to travel or if you find yourself off trail and uncertain of your surroundings, **STOP**.

If you end up where it's not smart or safe to go any farther, then bring people to you:

→ Call out or blow your whistle and listen for a response. Do this consistently, about every five minutes, but not to the point that you wear yourself out.

→ Continue to use your phone if you have a signal.

→ If you have the knowledge and equipment, and if it's safe to do so, start a small fire so the smoke will attract attention.

→ If you have a signal mirror, use it to alert any sky traffic to your location. A signal mirror is a small mirror with a hole in the middle. You use it to reflect light and send a signal to an aircraft that might be able to help with your rescue.

By using these strategies and staying on trail you are doing everything you can to be found as quickly as possible.

Choose a comfortable place and position on the trail. Stay directly on the trail if you can or in a highly visible area where it will be easy for your group to find you. Don't retreat to a cave or under a tree unless the weather is poor and there are no other options for protection. You will also want to wear brightly colored clothes if you have them to make it easier for other people to see you. If it is cold and you have a sleeping bag or extra clothes, then go ahead and layer up and crawl into the bag to stay warm. If there is precipitation and high winds and you have a tent or tarp, then go ahead and set it up to protect yourself from the elements. If you need to spend the night in the woods without camping gear, then pile up as many dry leaves or pine needles as possible to make a bed and then put more needles and leaves on top of you for warmth. You can also make a primitive shelter using sticks and branches.

If there are no high winds or precipitation and you are able to build a fire, then do so. Building a fire will help provide warmth and comfort; it will give you an activity to occupy your mind; and the smoke will hopefully lead the folks looking for you to your exact location.

Staying Calm and Comfortable

It's easy to stay comfortable in good weather, but it can be very difficult to remain comfortable and calm if you find yourself in pouring rain, snow, high winds, a record heat wave, or bug season. If it is freezing cold, you may need to do jumping jacks to stay warm. If it is blazing hot and sunny, you might have to hold a jacket over your head for shade.

TRY IT → Whistling for Help

Three blasts on a whistle means that you need help. It might take whoever hears your signal some time to get to you!

WHAT YOU'LL NEED

➢ Two whistles and a friend.

STEP 1 Go to a familiar park or trail. Separate from your friend and get into a position where you can't see the other person but can hear the whistle.

STEP 2 Practice whistling to each other. If you hear three quick whistle blasts, call out, "Do you need help?"

HELP!

STEP 3 Take turns whistling and responding to each other. (But whatever you do, don't practice this activity indoors or there is a very good chance that you will not have an emergency whistle to carry on your next hike.)

I DID IT! DATE:

Part of staying calm and comfortable in the woods is making a plan. Fill in the blanks below to help complete a plan for staying safe and comfortable and being found.

If I am hiking and find myself lost or separated from my group,

I will not .... I will remain calm.

I will also stay on the ....

I will call out for my group or other hikers who might be

close by. If I don't hear anything, I will blow my emergency

.... After I take a few deep

breaths, I will check my cell phone to see if I have service.

I will eat a snack and drink some water while I look at my

.... and see if I can figure out

where I am.

I DID IT! DATE:

TAKE IT TO THE NEXT LEVEL ↗

Volunteer to Be a Hero

Did you know that many of the individuals involved in backcountry search-and-rescue missions are volunteers? Research local search-and-rescue (SAR) teams to find out how to volunteer—maybe you can help find someone, too!

I DID IT! DATE:

LEAVE NO TRACE PRINCIPLES

101 ACHIEVEMENTS

INDEX

Leave No Trace Principles

Leave No Trace is an international movement, nonprofit organization, and educational program dedicated to protecting the outdoors by teaching people to enjoy it responsibly. The organization accomplishes this mission by delivering cutting-edge education and research to millions of people across the country every year. The organization uses seven science-based principles as its foundational tenets.

KNOW BEFORE YOU GO

- Be prepared! Don't forget clothes that protect you from cold, heat, and rain.
- Use maps to show you where you'll be going and so you won't get lost.
- Learn about the area you visit. Read books and talk to people before you go. The more you know, the more fun you'll have.

CHOOSE THE RIGHT PATH

- Stay on the main trail to protect nature and don't wander off by yourself.
- Steer clear of flowers or small trees. Once hurt, they may not grow back.
- Use existing camp areas and camp at least 100 big steps from roads, trails, and water.

TRASH YOUR TRASH

- Pack it in, Pack it out. Put litter, even crumbs, in trash cans or carry it home.
- Use bathrooms or outhouses when available. If you have to "go," act like a cat and bury poop in a small hole 4–8 inches deep and 100 big steps from water.
- Place your toilet paper in a plastic bag and put the bag in a garbage can back home.
- Keep water clean. Do not put soap, food, or poop in lakes or streams.

LEAVE WHAT YOU FIND

- Leave plants, rocks, and historical items as you find them so the next person can enjoy them. Treat living plants with respect. Hacking or peeling plants can kill them.
- Good campsites are found, not made. Don't dig trenches or build structures in your campsite.

BE CAREFUL WITH FIRE

- Use a camp stove for cooking. It's easier to cook on and clean up than a fire.
- Be sure it's OK to build a campfire in the area you're visiting. Use an existing fire ring to protect the ground from heat. Keep your fire small. Remember, campfires aren't for trash or food.
- Do not snap branches off live, dead, or downed trees. Instead, collect loose sticks from the ground.
- Burn all wood to ash and be sure that the fire is completely out and cold before you leave.

RESPECT WILDLIFE

- Observe animals from a distance and never approach, feed or follow them. Human food is unhealthy for all animals and feeding them starts bad habits.
- Protect wildlife and your food by storing your meals and trash.
- Control pets at all times, or leave them at home.

BE KIND TO OTHER VISITORS

- Make sure the fun you have outdoors does not bother anyone else. Remember that other visitors are there to enjoy the outdoors.
- Listen to nature. Avoid making loud noises or yelling. You will see more animals if you are quiet.

**Remember—you'll enjoy nature even more
by caring for your special place.**

**For more information, please contact Leave No Trace.
1.800.332.4100 or www.LNT.org**

101 OUTDOOR SCHOOL
HIKING AND CAMPING ACHIEVEMENTS

The outdoors are calling—and this is the list of everything they have to offer. Track everything you master, experience, and collect on your adventures by checking off your achievements below. See if you can complete all 101!

1. Calculated hiking pace
2. Made a rain poncho
3. Cooked a meal with a camping stove
4. Filtered safe drinking water
5. Assembled a first aid kit
6. Completed a wilderness first aid course
7. Gathered the Ten Essentials
8. Practiced signaling for help
9. Had a campfire sing-along
10. Made meals for a one-day hike
11. Made meals for a multi-day hike
12. Used a natural refrigerator on the trail

13. Skipped rocks on a lake
14. Had a picnic on a hike
15. Made your own trail mix or dehydrated fruit
16. Hiked a stop-and-smell hike
17. Hiked a slow-and-steady hike
18. Hiked a challenge-style hike
19. Tried trail running
20. Joined an outdoor club or expedition group
21. Went on a night hike
22. Found north, south, east, and west on a hike
23. Identified the Big Dipper with Polaris (the North star)
24. Used shadows to navigate during a day hike

25 Sketched a bird

26 Played a trail game

27 Hiked with a topographic map

28 Hiked with a compass

29 Used a compass to map your backyard or local park

30 Found hidden cache

31 Used and recorded a hike with a GPS

32 Used a geocaching app to hide a new geocache

33 Found latitude and longitude on a hike

34 Hiked in an area with little shade

35 Practiced an ice self-arrest

36 Practiced river crossing techniques

37 Hunted for water on a hike

38 Practiced the lightning safety position

39 Spotted three different types of lightning

40 Went on a waterfall hike

41 Spotted a rainbow at a waterfall

42 Heard an owl screech

43 Went on a device-free hike

44 Identified a tree by a wind sound

45 Identified a tree by its bark texture

46 Identified an animal by sound

46 Identified a bird by its call

48 Used a naturalist animal sighting app

49 Played the color matching nature challenge

50 Went on a salamander hunt

51 Identified an animal by its tracks

52 Created a unique campfire game

53 Set up a campsite in the dark

54 Set up a tent

55 Set up an A-frame, diamond, or lean-to tarp

56 Watched synchronous fireflies

57 Identified igneous, sedimentary, and metamorphic rock

58 Learned the bowline and two-half-hitch knots

59 Went on a meditation hike

60 Constructed a fire ring

61 Built and put out a fire

62 Hung a bear bag

63 Spotted animals in three different habitats

64 Practiced visualization for emergencies

65 Heard a coyote yip or howl

66 Completed a tick check

67 Researched poisonous plants and animals in my area

68 Practiced writing a SOAP note

69 Heard cicadas

70 Went on a microclimate safari

71 Made a signal mirror

72 Volunteered with a local search-and-rescue (SAR) team

73 Went on a habitat scavenger hunt

74 Spotted and recorded three different animals on a hike

75 Made a casting of an animal track

76 Went on an insect-spotting hike

77 Went on a bird-spotting hike

78 Went on a bird-nest-spotting hike

79 Pressed three different types of leaves

80 Went on a tree-spotting hike

81 Went on a wildflower safari

82 Made spore prints

83 Identified three different rock formations on a hike

84 Planned three go-to hikes

85 Created a bucket list of wild animals to see

86 Set up a makeshift campsite

87 Set up a tarp without poles in an area without trees

88 Hiked through a natural arch

89 Went on a winter-tree-spotting hike

90 Learned the Latin names of five flowers

91 Went on a mushroom-spotting hike

92 Made home-grown mushrooms

93 Made three different fossils

94 Went on a rock-spotting hike

95 Completed a CPR course

96 Identified an animal by its scat

97 Found a geode

98 Created shade on a sunny day

99 Watched an animal or insect hunt

100 Created a plan for being found

101 Spotted a glacial erratic

INDEX